Body Image & Self-Esteem

Editor: Danielle Lobban

Volume 446

First published by Independence Educational Publishers
The Studio, High Green
Great Shelford
Cambridge CB22 5EG
England

© Independence 2024

Copyright

This book is sold subject to the condition that it shall not,
by way of trade or otherwise, be lent, resold, hired out or otherwise
circulated in any form of binding or cover other than that in which it
is published without the publisher's prior consent.

Photocopy licence

The material in this book is protected by copyright. However, the
purchaser is free to make multiple copies of particular articles for instructional
purposes for immediate use within the purchasing institution.
Making copies of the entire book is not permitted.

ISBN-13: 978 1 86168 906 1

Printed in Great Britain
Pureprint Group

Acknowledgements

The publisher is grateful for permission to reproduce the material in this book. While every care has been taken to trace and acknowledge copyright, the publisher tenders its apology for any accidental infringement or where copyright has proved untraceable. The publisher would be pleased to come to a suitable arrangement in any such case with the rightful owner.

The material reproduced in **issues** books is provided as an educational resource only. The views, opinions and information contained within reprinted material in **issues** books do not necessarily represent those of Independence Educational Publishers and its employees.

Although every effort has been made to ensure that website addresses are correct at time of going to press, Independence Educational Publishers cannot be held responsible for the content of any website mentioned in this book.

Images

Cover image courtesy of iStock. All other images courtesy of Freepik, Pixabay, Pexels, and Unsplash.

Additional acknowledgements

With thanks to the Independence team: Janey Hills, Klaudia Sommer and Jackie Staines.

Danielle Lobban

Cambridge, October 2024

Contents

Chapter 1: Body Image

What is body image?	1
The 4 components of body image	2
7 factors influencing your body image	4
Body image statistics 2024: 50+ shocking facts	5
Body dysmorphic disorder (BDD)	9
More than my mental health: Body Dysmorphic Disorder	11
Male body dysmorphia is a modern epidemic that's only worsening	14
Body image issues affect close to 40% of men – but many don't get the support they need	16
Exploring the dangers of idealised masculinity	18
Show don't tell: parents' role in promoting positive body image	19
Body image in childhood	20

Chapter 2: Body Image and The Media

Children and negative body image: are filters to blame?	22
The media, fashion companies and the pressure of having a perfect body	24
'Not much has changed': how fashion rules body image	26
Social media is tanking people's body image	28
The camera never lies…	30
Artificial Intelligence, body image and toxic expectations	32
New project to help young women deal with social media body image pressures	34

Chapter 3: Feeling Positive!

Body positivity: embracing every body	35
Body positivity – why women are tired of skinny stereotypes	36
Where is the male body positivity movement?	38
How to deal with body image issues	40

Further Reading/Useful Websites	42
Glossary	43
Index	44

Introduction

Body Image & Self-Esteem is volume 446 in the **issues** series. The aim of the series is to offer current, diverse information about important issues in our world, from a UK perspective.

About *Body Image & Self-Esteem*

Over a third of adults have felt anxious or depressed because of their body image. But what can make people feel this way? This book examines reasons for poor body image, such as influences from the media, confidence issues, and how to have a positive body image.

Our sources

Titles in the **issues** series are designed to function as educational resource books, providing a balanced overview of a specific subject.

The information in our books is comprised of facts, articles and opinions from many different sources, including:

- Newspaper reports and opinion pieces
- Website factsheets
- Magazine and journal articles
- Statistics and surveys
- Government reports
- Literature from special interest groups.

A note on critical evaluation

Because the information reprinted here is from a number of different sources, readers should bear in mind the origin of the text and whether the source is likely to have a particular bias when presenting information (or when conducting their research). It is hoped that, as you read about the many aspects of the issues explored in this book, you will critically evaluate the information presented.

It is important that you decide whether you are being presented with facts or opinions. Does the writer give a biased or unbiased report? If an opinion is being expressed, do you agree with the writer? Is there potential bias to the 'facts' or statistics behind an article?

Activities

Throughout this book, you will find a selection of assignments and activities designed to help you engage with the articles you have been reading and to explore your own opinions. Some tasks will take longer than others and there is a mixture of design, writing and research-based activities that you can complete alone or in a group.

Further research

At the end of each article we have listed its source and a website that you can visit if you would like to conduct your own research. Please remember to critically evaluate any sources that you consult and consider whether the information you are viewing is accurate and unbiased.

Issues Online

The **issues** series of books is complemented by our online resource, issuesonline.co.uk

On the Issues Online website you will find a wealth of information, covering over 75 topics, to support the PSHE and RSE curriculum.

Why Issues Online?

Researching a topic? Issues Online is the best place to start for…

Librarians

Issues Online is an essential tool for librarians: feel confident you are signposting safe, reliable, user-friendly online resources to students and teaching staff alike. We provide multi-user concurrent access, so no waiting around for another student to finish with a resource. Issues Online also provides FREE downloadable posters for your shelf/wall/table displays.

Teachers

Issues Online is an ideal resource for lesson planning, inspiring lively debate in class, and setting lessons and homework tasks.

Our accessible, engaging content helps deepen students' knowledge, promotes critical thinking, and develops independent learning skills.

Issues Online saves precious preparation time. We wade through the wealth of material on the internet to filter the best quality, most relevant and up-to-date information you need to start exploring a topic.

Our carefully selected, balanced content presents an overview and insight into each topic from a variety of sources and viewpoints.

Students

Issues Online is designed to support your studies in a broad range of topics, particularly social issues relevant to young people today.

There are thousands of articles, statistics and infographs instantly available to help you with homework, research, and assignments.

With 24/7 access using the powerful Algolia search system, you can find relevant information quickly, easily and safely anytime from your laptop, tablet or smartphone, in class or at home.

Visit issuesonline.co.uk to find out more!

Chapter 1

Body Image

What is body image?

Have you ever stood in front of a mirror and felt a flurry of mixed emotions about what you see? Well, you're not alone. This feeling is part of something much bigger, something we call body image. In simple terms, body image is how we see ourselves when we look in the mirror or when we picture ourselves in our minds. It encompasses what we believe about our appearance including our memories, assumptions, and generalisations. Teenagers often feel like they are sailing through a stormy sea when it comes to body image.

Understanding and cultivating a healthy body image is crucial during these formative years, as it can significantly impact your self-esteem and overall wellbeing.

Understanding body image

Body image is not just about how we perceive our physical appearance but also how we feel about our bodies. It comprises two main components:

- **Perceptual body image:** how we see our body and how accurately we perceive our size and shape.
- **Affective body image:** our feelings about our body's appearance.

The media, our peers, and societal standards play a pivotal role in shaping our body image. They often bombard us with images and ideas of what's considered 'perfect' or 'ideal,' leading to unrealistic expectations. It's vital to recognise these influences and discern the common misconceptions. Remember, not everything we see online or in media is the complete truth.

Body image and self-esteem

Body image and self-esteem are closely intertwined. A positive body image can boost your self-esteem, making you feel confident and proud of who you are. On the flip side, a negative body image can lead to a drop in self-worth. Here's how you can work on improving both:

- Focus on your qualities: Recognise and celebrate your strengths and achievements.
- Surround yourself with positivity: Engage with friends and communities that uplift you.
- Positive representation matters: Look for and support media that showcases diverse and realistic images of bodies.

Impact of body image on mental health

Negative body image can significantly affect your mental health, leading to stress, anxiety, depression, and even eating disorders. Recognising these risks is step one. If you're struggling, don't hesitate to seek help from a trusted adult or professional. Coping strategies include:

- Mindfulness and self-compassion: Practice being kind to yourself.
- Professional help: Never shy away from seeking therapy or counselling.

Promoting a healthy body image

Developing a healthy body image is a journey, not a destination. Here are some practical steps you can take:

- Practice self-care: Engage in activities that make you feel good about yourself, physically and emotionally.
- Positive self-talk: Challenge negative thoughts about your body with positive affirmations.
- Embrace your uniqueness: Celebrate the things that make you, uniquely you.

Body positivity and diversity

The body positivity movement is about embracing all bodies, regardless of size, shape, or appearance, asserting that every body is beautiful. Real-life examples of body positivity can be found in activists like Jameela Jamil and models like Ashley Graham, who advocate for self-love and acceptance. Through diversifying our feeds and supporting inclusive brands and media, we can begin to appreciate the beauty in diversity.

Body image is a complex part of our self-view, influenced by numerous external and internal factors. As teenagers, it's essential to question and understand these influences, fostering a healthy and positive relationship with our bodies. Remember, your worth is not defined by your appearance. Embrace your unique self, and let self-love be your guiding force. Keep exploring the topic of body image and self-acceptance, for it's a vital step towards living a happier, healthier life.

Body image issues are a common struggle, but with the right support and strategies, anyone can work towards a healthier, more positive self-image. Remember, your journey is yours, and you are not alone.

The 4 components of body image

Your body image creates the relationship you have with your body.

By Monica Johnson Psy.D.

It's the start of a new year, and for many, that means standing in front of the mirror, cataloguing everything that is 'wrong' with your body that you plan to fix this year. Well, I'm here to help you fix your mind about your body!

We will start by giving a basic definition of body image. Your body image encompasses your perceptions, beliefs, feelings, thoughts, and actions that pertain to your physical appearance. In essence, it's your personal relationship with your body. I like this definition because you have a lot of control over those things if you're using the right coping strategies.

The goal in my mind is to spend most of our time in a body positive or body neutral state. There is enormous societal pressure to look a certain way, so even the best of us will have insecurities that crop up from time to time.

Examples of negative body image

When people have a negative body image, there are many ways that manifests. We can be avoidant; for example, performing behaviours like avoiding buying new clothes or looking into mirrors, or intentionally trying to hide parts of our bodies. How many of you hide your bellies or refuse to wear shorts because you have thicker thighs or cellulite? All this does is communicate the message that your body is bad. The first time I wore a two-piece swimsuit, I was close to 400 lbs. I was inspired by Gabifresh, who had dropped on the scene as a fashion blogger and eventually started her own swimsuit line. It was liberating to let it all hang out. We are four-dimensional beings and it's okay if our curves reflect that. Everything from a Megan Thee Stallion to Alfred Hitchcock silhouette is welcome!

Another negative body image style is conflictual. Are you constantly battling with your body and telling it that it needs to be something that it's not? Does *I Wish* by Skee-Lo constantly ring in your head? Do you think if you were a little taller, that woman you're crushing on would notice you? Do you have curly hair and wish it was straight? Or straight hair and wish it was curly? Are you more on the slender slide and want to be bigger?

Embrace yourself instead of trying to replace everything that makes you a unique human being. Fun fact, I was born with seven birthmarks, one of which covers almost a third of my torso. I remember being in junior high and wishing that I had unmarked skin like every other girl I saw. If you looked at my yearbooks from high school, I wore a jacket every day – and I grew up in South Carolina, y'all! Now, I make off-colour jokes about how I could never join a secret society or that if I ended up the victim in a true crime story, my body would be super identifiable. What changed? Those birthmarks are still there, but my perception changed over time, which is a key aspect of body image. More on that in a minute.

Another type of negative body image is abusive. Do you have an abusive relationship with your body? Do you call yourself names? Starve yourself? Exercise to the point of exhaustion? Do you engage in self-harm? These are all examples of the ways we can be abusive to ourselves. I would never condone anyone being abusive, including self-abusive.

Now, let's talk about the four aspects of body image.

Perceptual

Perceptual body image is how you see yourself. The way that you see your body is not always a correct representation of what you actually look like – it's a perception, not the objective truth. For example, a person may perceive themselves to be fat when in reality they are underweight. You could have a small mole on your nose and perceive yourself as an ugly witch while the rest of us barely notice it.

Perception is a tricky beast. I routinely tell my friends that I have what I've deemed to be 'fat girl brain.' What does that mean? I perceive myself as though I'm still over 400 lbs – my reality until a few years ago. I will look at a chair and think, 'I can't fit in that space,' or walk by a mirror and stop and legitimately have the thought 'that's what I look like?' In the same way that the hand is quicker than the eye, change is often quicker than perception.

That's why with perception, you need to have an act first, feel later approach. If you want your perception to match reality, mindfulness is your friend. The judgmental statements that we make about ourselves keep our perceptual lens distorted. If I sit down and I have rolls in my belly and I appraise that as meaning 'I'm fat,' then I will see myself as

fat. If I acknowledge their presence and the fact that it's totally normal, I can change my experience over time. I'm confident that Zendaya has thigh spread just like the rest of us, and she's on magazine covers.

Affective

Your feelings about your body, especially the amount of satisfaction or dissatisfaction you experience in relation to your appearance (e.g., weight, body shape, height, skin tone, aging, etc.) is your affective body image. These are all the things that you like or dislike about yourself.

Obviously, these feelings are influenced by our societal consumptions: who we see on TV, in movies, in magazines, and, more recently, social media. Are you only following Instagram models who are Facetuned and Photoshopped into a digitally inaccurate representation of the person? Stop that! Introduce body image diversity into your life. It's important to make a conscious decision about the media you consume and the effect it has on you, both positive and negative.

Sometimes, we come from cultures that influence these ideas. For instance, I'm Black, and the idealisation of large backsides is a part of my culture. Guess who doesn't have a large butt? Me. Does it make me less Black or my body image less positive overall? No. Do I welcome the Bulgarian Squats that my trainer has me do because I have a small hope of getting a slightly more rotund gluteus maximus? Yes! Will I be Megan Thee Stallion? No. Does it change my value as a person? Also, no!

Hating yourself is not a requirement for change. You can be dissatisfied by something AND accepting of it at the same time. So, for all my no-booty Black people out there – or really anyone of any race – unite! If you're going to do comparisons, at least do ones that allow you to feel included and not ones that make you feel ostracised. This will help to improve your body image over time.

Cognitive

These are the thoughts and beliefs that you hold about your body.

You might be a guy who thinks, 'if I become more muscular, I'll feel better about myself.' Or maybe you're a woman in her 30s who is afraid of aging and thinks, 'if I can just maintain how I look now I'll be happy!' If/then contingencies like this often add up to maybe/never in my experience. If you inherently dislike yourself, you'll move the goal post. You'll lose 20 lbs and then say, 'I just need to lose another 10.'

In my last episode, I spoke about the importance of your values and the why when you're goal setting. I've seen many people change their bodies and never be mentally satisfied with the progress. There is always a little more weight to lose, a little more muscle to gain, and a grey hair that shows up that wasn't there before. Set positive, health-focused goals, rather than ones based on unrealistic standards.

If you're born with a Chris Rock body type, it's unlikely you'll end up being The Rock. If you set that up as the goal, you may be setting yourself up for failure. Does that mean you can't put on mass and increase your musculature? Absolutely not! Just be realistic with yourself about what that looks like. And instead of trying to avoid aging altogether, perhaps you should define for yourself what aging gracefully looks like. We may need to embrace a few grey hairs and wrinkles in order to not end up on an episode of *Botched* someday.

Behavioural

The last aspect of body image is behavioural. This is what you do in relation to your body image. When a person doesn't like how they look, they may employ destructive behaviours. This can be anything from excessive exercise habits to disordered eating as a means to change their appearance. Others might isolate themselves or not engage in pleasant events because of their body image.

One of my favourite tips is to focus on the function of your body. If you want to engage in more hikes but you're out of shape right now, great! Choose easier hikes and work your way up to more difficult ones. That's focusing on function.

Your body is amazing! Whether you're an atheist or devout Catholic, our shared experience is that we have these bodies that allow us to be connected to this world. These bodies take damage from the elements, let us taste a juicy cheeseburger, run marathons, dance, and make love. Every single thing I just listed can be done by any body type at any age – with a few modifications, of course.

If you change your mind about your body, you remove the limits on what your current body and self can experience. In that way, you can craft an existence of self-acceptance and start living the way you desire.

2022

The above information is reprinted with kind permission from Quick & Dirty Tips™
© 2024 Macmillan Publishing Group, LLC

www.quickanddirtytips.com

7 factors influencing your body image

By Harriet Frew, MSc; MBACP Accred

The development of your body image begins from birth. Many unconscious and conscious messages become woven into your psyche, these then influencing your beliefs and perceptions about your body.

1. The culture

In Western culture, there is a definite preference towards a thinner physique, for women. This preference became particularly amplified in the 1960s, with slender models such as Twiggy, celebrated widely. This trend accelerated through the 1980s with women's magazines, the promotion of diets and the increased focus on body shape and manipulating it. It could be argued that it reached its peak (pre-social media) in the 1990s, in the era of waif-like super-models, such as Kate Moss.

Since the 2000s, with many more TV channels and the advent of social media, the access to and daily bombardment of idealised images has taken over to such a degree that you can be overwhelmed 24/7.

Men are increasingly targeted and impacted too, with the pressure to conform to an athletic and muscular physique.

The latest incarnation of the ideal body has been towards clean eating and chasing a lean physique – #fitspo. On the surface, it might appear to be a healthier version of the old ideal, but the underlying conditionality of the message prevails.

In the media, we still do not see a true cross-section and representation of human bodies. There is a distinct lack of representation of people of different race, disability, sexuality, and age. This impacts our preference for what is appealing in a body. We have been taught to like the white, young and thin female.

Thankfully, there is some backlash against these old limiting ideals, with people promoting body positivity and health at every size (HAES). There is still a very long way to go, though.

2. Self-esteem

Having a healthy self-esteem is very preventative against negative body image. Healthy self-esteem offers a thicker skin and protection against external messages. You will buy-in less and have more objectivity to the toxic cultural preferences. You will feel less need to conform to the ideal, to boost self-esteem, as worth is rooted internally, rather than chasing external approval and validation.

3. Family values and attitudes

If you had a parent who constantly dieted or was unhappy with their shape, they will have inadvertently passed on many messages to you. Additionally, if your parents often commented about the weight and shape of others or were fatphobic, you will have likely internalised these messages also.

Sibling rivalry can sometimes fuel negative body image. If someone is particularly blessed genetically and overtly praised for this, the self-esteem of the other siblings can suffer.

If your self-esteem is low within the family group and you have been criticised or judged regularly (not just about appearance but other factors), you will be more vulnerable to being harsh on yourself about weight and shape too.

4. Abuse or trauma

If you have experienced trauma, assault or abuse then, unsurprisingly, this can have a momentous impact on your body image. Early trauma can be held in the body and can lead to feelings of unworthiness or unacceptability. Focusing on changing your body can be a way to dissociate or numb from the painful underlying feelings, although this process may be entirely unconscious.

5. Puberty

Particularly in women, puberty can be a trigger for negative body image. If you develop earlier than your peers or received unwanted attention in relation to your appearance, this can create troubling feelings about your body. If you experience a noticeable change in height or weight during puberty, this can heighten feelings of discomfort or self-consciousness.

6. Physical activity

Playing sports and being active is often beneficial for body image. However, if there is pressure to conform to a certain body shape e.g., fitness competitions, ballet or horse-racing as examples, this can increase body preoccupation and dissatisfaction.

7. Acceptance or rejection in relation to your body

If you have been endlessly praised about your appearance, interestingly, this can lead to greater body dissatisfaction and feeling pressured to maintain your looks. It can create objectification or envy from others.

If you have been criticised or rejected for how you look, this also has an understandable profound impact. Bullying of all kinds is incredibly harmful and this can lead to longstanding emotional wounds and self-consciousness, often projected onto the body.

Understanding how your body image has developed can offer valuable reflection and insights. It offers you an opportunity to step back and then to offer yourself understanding and compassion. Body positivity might not be a realistic goal for everyone but, certainly, respect and appreciation for your body can be realistic goals to work towards.

If you are struggling with your body image, you might want to seek out further support through counselling.

20 January 2021

The above information is reprinted with kind permission from Counselling Directory.
© 2024 Happiful

www.counselling-directory.org.uk

Body image statistics 2024: 50+ shocking facts

By Dr Jake Linardon

Body image problems need to be taken seriously. And in 2024, now more than ever.

Body image problems are one of the strongest risk factors for the development of an eating disorder, not to mention that they also lead to other unhealthy weight control behaviours.

Read on as we share a number of shocking statistics and facts about body image.

What is body image?

Body image refers to how we think about, feel and act towards our body. It is a multifaceted construct, meaning that it consists of many different perceptual, attitudinal, and behavioural components.

Negative body image can cause so many negative outcomes, like:

- Depressive and anxiety symptomology
- Increased risk of suicidal thoughts
- Low self-esteem
- Interpersonal problems
- Alcohol and drug use and abuse
- Reduced physical activity
- Loss of sex drive
- Stress
- Social isolation
- Decreased motivation to seek help
- Perfectionistic tendencies
- Repetitive negative thoughts

Key terms

There are so many different elements of body image.

We need to clarify what each of these components means before jumping straight into the statistics related to these components.

- Body dissatisfaction: a general unhappiness with your body or its parts.
- Overvaluation of weight/shape: basing who you are as a person almost entirely on what you look like or what the number on the scales tells you.
- Body preoccupation: obsessively thinking or ruminating about what your body weighs or what it looks like.
- Body checking: repeatedly check your weight and shape, through behaviours like self-weighing, staring in the mirror, comparing yourself with others, or pinching your body parts to assess for fat and muscle.
- Body image avoidance: avoiding situations that can elicit concerns about your body, like a refusal to be weighed, wearing baggy clothes as a 'disguise', or the covering up of mirrors.
- Feeling fat: a somatic sensation that you are carrying more fat than what you actually hold in reality, irrespective of actual body mass.
- Fear of weight gain: irrational, illogical, and harmful fears that you're gaining weight.
- Thin-ideal internalisation: buying into the belief that being thin will make you happy, popular, or successful.
- Body dysmorphia: a body image disorder characterised by the obsessive idea that some aspect of one's own body part is profoundly flawed and hence warrants behaviours designed to hide or fix these perceived flaws.
- Muscle dysmorphia: a body image disorder that centrally comprises a core belief and fear around being of insufficient muscularity, and a simultaneous drive for muscularity.

Now that you understand some common terminology, let's turn to some key statistics on body image in men and women.

Body image statistics for adults

1. More than 50% of adults from the US, UK, Australia, France and Germany reported experiencing weight stigma.
2. 11% of women, 25% of men, and 18% of gender diverse Canadian adolescents reported clinical risk of muscle dysmorphia.
3. Nearly one in three health club users reported significant symptoms of body dysmorphia, of which 70% of these had an eating disorder.
4. 1.6% of young adults report using androgenic-anabolic steroids as a means to modify their appearance.
5. Adults who used anabolic steroids for body image purposes are three to four times more likely to experience depression and anxiety than those who don't use steroids.

Body image statistics for men

Children and teenagers

6. Research conducted in the US showed that around 25% of male children/adolescents were concerned about their muscularity and leanness, by expressing a greater desire for toned and defined muscles.
7. 36% of students from United Arab Emirates report being dissatisfied with their body.
8. From a sample of 3,618 Australian adolescents, 2.2% of boys an 1.2% of girls reported the presence of muscle dysmorphia.
9. From a sample of Australian adolescents, 6.8% of boys and 19.6% of girls reported clinically significant body dissatisfaction.
10. Research on Australian male children and adolescents reported that around 17% were dissatisfied with their body and that around 5% reported an overvaluation of weight/shape.
11. Body dysmorphic disorder symptoms are becoming increasingly common in male teenagers, with nearly 3% of the Australian population reporting body dysmorphic symptoms.
12. In 15,624 American high school students, 30% of males reported a desire to gain weight for muscularity purposes.
13. Around 17% of adolescent boys perceived themselves to be underweight, despite being of normal weight.
14. Multiracial and African American adolescent boys were nearly two times more likely to attempt weight gain than Caucasian adolescent boys.
15. Of 4,701 adolescent boys, 23% reported engaging in unhealthy muscle building behaviour at 1-year follow-up, with this figure increasing to 30% at 7-year follow-up.
16. Among Australian adolescent boys, 12% met criteria for an eating disorder characterised by marked body image disturbances.
17. Around 20% of German child/adolescent boys felt fat, 15% were terrified of gaining weight, and 25% reported regularly feeling upset about weight or shape.
18. 20% of adolescents with diabetes report significant dissatisfaction with their body shape.
19. More than 90% of young people in Australia have some concern about their body image.
20. One in two (50%) young Australians said that how they view their body has prevented them at some point from raising their hand in class.
21. Over a third (37%) of young Australians admitted that their body image stopped them from participating in physical activity or sport quite a bit or all of the time.
22. More than a third (36%) of young Australians confirmed their body image stopped them from giving an opinion or standing up for themselves.

23. For student-athletes in the NCAA, 68% of men and 45% of women felt they have a good body, 53% of men and 35% of women were happy with their current weight, and 59% of men and 31% of women liked what they look like in pictures.

Males: adult men

24. Nearly 15% of Australian men report an overvaluation of weight and shape.
25. Three quarters of young boys/men report using appearance- and performance-enhancing substances to modify their body image.
26. In US adult men, 9% reported frequent body checking and 5% reported body image avoidance.
27. In a sample of French university students, more than 85% of the men samples were dissatisfied with their muscularity.
28. Nearly 2% of German male population met diagnostic criteria for body dysmorphic disorder, and more than 2.5% are expected to exhibit clinically significant levels of muscle dysphoria.
29. Nearly 22% of young men report engaging in muscle-enhancing behaviours, including eating more or differently to build muscle(17%), supplement use (7%), and androgenic-anabolic steroid use (3%).
30. 15% of young men with BMI at least 25 report engaging in disordered eating behaviours, including fasting, skipping meals, vomiting, laxatives, diuretics, or binge-eating.
31. 8% of young men with BMI less than 25 report engaging in these disordered eating behaviours.
32. In more than 50,000 adults, 41% of men thought they were too heavy and were self-conscious about their weight, 16% reported being too uncomfortable in a swimsuit, and 11% thought that they were unattractive.

Body image statistics for women

Children and teenagers

33. Research has shown that around 50% of young 13-year-old American girls reported being unhappy with their body. This number grew to nearly 80% by the time girls reached 17 years of age.
34. Nearly 80% of young teenage girls report fears of becoming fat.
35. Among adolescents who believed they 'weren't thin enough' or 'might get too fat', 53% exhibited clinical symptoms of body dysmorphic disorder.
36. In German adolescent girls, nearly one-third perceived a BMI of less than 18 to be the ideal female body size.
37. A total of 36% of German child/adolescent girls felt fat, 22% were terrified of gaining weight, and 36% reported regularly feeling upset about their weight or shape.
38. In 657 Spanish girls, nearly 50% expressed a desire for a thinner body, despite being of a normal body weight.
39. In the same sample of Spanish girls, nearly 90% of girls who were overweight expressed a desire for a thinner body, and only 11% wanted their body to stay the same.
40. Body image was listed in the top four concerns for young women.

Females: adult women

41. Nearly one in two adult women report feeling more concerned with the way they look during the pandemic lockdown.
42. In one Switzerland study of 1,000 adult women (aged 30–74 years), despite 73% of women falling within the normal weight range, more than 70% of these women expressed a desire to be thinner.
43. This trend also held true for older women (>65 years); 65% were of normal weight, yet 62% of these women wished to be thinner.
44. Around 60% of elderly women (aged 60–70 years) in Austria are dissatisfied with their body and more than half reported restricting their eating as a means to prevent weight gain.
45. In US adult women, 23% reported frequent body checking and 11% reported body image avoidance.
46. One large cohort study reported no differences in rates of body dissatisfaction between Caucasian and African-American adult women, with around 50% of the women from each group reporting body dissatisfaction.
47. Nearly 23% of Australian women report an overvaluation of weight and shape.
48. Nearly 70% of adult women report withdrawing from activities due to their body image.
49. In more than 50,000 adults, 60% of women thought they were too heavy and were self-conscious about their weight, 30% reported being too uncomfortable in a swimsuit, and 20% thought that they were unattractive.
50. In a sample of 160 African American adult women, 47% were dissatisfied with their body image, 11% felt that they were unattractive, and 75% were somewhat unsatisfied with their weight.

Media influence on body image

The media can have a negative influence on body image.

In fact, a good deal of experimental research has shown that the media can actually cause people to feel unhappy with their body.

How then does the media cause body dissatisfaction?

The media is full of promoting unrealistic ideals about what men and women's body type should look like in order to be considered attractive.

Unfortunately, due to basic biology these ideals are largely unattainable. So, people who buy into the mantra that thin/muscular is synonymous with beauty, popularity, and success are often left feeling sad, ashamed, and unhappy with their body.

The consequence of this is that these people will then go to great lengths to try and achieve this seemingly unrealistic ideal by engaging in harmful weight control behaviours, like extreme dieting, or taking steroids, laxatives, or diuretics.

All of these behaviours have the potential to cause an eating disorder.

Let's turn our attention to some specific studies that have looked at the role of the media on body dissatisfaction, and discuss some of their key findings and statistics.

There is a great deal of evidence showing that mainstream media outlets continuously promote the notion that thinness is equated with numerous positive outcomes. Some interesting findings include:

51. A study in 2004 that identified the top 25 children videos found that more than two-thirds of these videos linked thinness and physical attractiveness with positive personality traits (e.g., caring, kindness) while 75% of the videos linked obesity with unfavourable traits.

52. These depictions were even more exaggerated in 2010, with 87% of female characters portrayed as underweight in over 180 popular children cartoon programs.

53. In another study of popular children cartoons, females were four times more likely than male characters to be depicted as underweight, and overweight characters were more likely to be portrayed as unintelligent and unhappy compared to underweight characters.

Let's now look at some data showing what specific impact the media has on people's body image concerns.

54. In one study of young girls aged between 13–17 years, nearly 50% reported a desire to be as skinny as the models they viewed in fashion magazines and reported that these magazines gave them a body to strive for.

55. Simply viewing a Barbie doll has been shown to reduce body esteem and increase a desire for thinness in girls aged 5–8 years.

56. A survey of 548 adolescent girls found that 69% acknowledged that images in magazines had influenced their conception of the ideal body weight, while 47% reported that they wanted to lose weight after seeing such images.

57. Girls who frequently read glamour magazines related to weight loss are six times more likely to engage in extreme unhealthy weight control behaviours (e.g., taking diet pills, using laxatives, vomiting) than girls who do not read such magazines.

Strategies for safe social media use

Unfollow! Unfollow or unlike pages that may be triggering or encouraging comparison making.
See how you go for a few days and observe whether you notice any changes in your perceptions, attitudes, and behaviours toward your body.

Seek out body positivity!
Make a conscious effort to follow or like body positivity pages. Being involved in a forum where all body shapes and sizes are respected will make you feel included and better about yourself.

Educate yourself.
Understand how social media works, how people interact with it, and the various ways social media content is manipulated. Always remind yourself that social media posts are rarely a true reflection of reality. This will enable you to be more compassionate towards yourself.

58. After television became widespread in Fiji, 11% of adolescent girls reported vomiting for weight control, 74% reported that they sometimes felt 'too big or fat', and the prevalence of disordered eating doubled from 13% to 29%.

59. One study found using social media for as little as 30 minutes a day can negatively change the way young women view their own body.

18 May 2024

Design
Design a poster displaying one of the facts in this article.

Think!
Choose three facts that are the most important or shocking to you.

The above information is reprinted with kind permission from Break Binge Eating.
© 2024 Break Binge Eating

www.breakbingeeating.com

Body dysmorphic disorder (BDD)

Body dysmorphic disorder (BDD), or body dysmorphia, is a mental health condition where a person spends a lot of time worrying about flaws in their appearance. These flaws are often unnoticeable to others.

People of any age can have BDD, but it's most common in teenagers and young adults. It affects both men and women.

Having BDD does not mean you're vain or self-obsessed. It can be very upsetting and have a big impact on your life.

Symptoms of body dysmorphic disorder

You might have body dysmorphic disorder (BDD) if you:

- worry a lot about a specific area of your body (particularly your face)
- spend a lot of time comparing your looks with other people's
- look at yourself in mirrors a lot or avoid mirrors altogether
- go to a lot of effort to conceal flaws – for example, by spending a long time combing your hair, applying make-up or choosing clothes
- pick at your skin to make it 'smooth'

BDD can seriously affect your daily life, including your work, social life and relationships.

BDD can also lead to depression, self-harm and even thoughts of suicide.

Getting help for body dysmorphic disorder

You should see a GP if you think you might have BDD.

They'll probably ask a number of questions about your symptoms and how they affect your life.

They may also ask if you've had any thoughts about harming yourself.

You may be treated by the GP, or they may refer you to a mental health specialist for further assessment and treatment.

It can be very difficult to seek help for BDD, but it's important to remember that you have nothing to feel ashamed or embarrassed about.

Getting help is important because your symptoms probably will not go away without treatment and may get worse.

You can also refer yourself directly to an NHS talking therapies service without a referral from a GP.

Treatments for body dysmorphic disorder

The symptoms of body dysmorphic disorder (BDD) can get better with treatment.

If your symptoms are relatively mild, you should be referred for a type of talking therapy called cognitive behavioural therapy (CBT), which you have either on your own or in a group.

If you have moderate symptoms, you should be offered either CBT or a type of antidepressant medicine called a selective serotonin reuptake inhibitor (SSRI).

If your symptoms are more severe, or other treatments do not work, you should be offered CBT together with an SSRI.

Cognitive behavioural therapy (CBT)

CBT can help you manage your BDD symptoms by changing the way you think and behave.

It helps you learn what triggers your symptoms, and teaches you different ways of thinking about and dealing with your habits.

You and your therapist will agree on goals for the therapy and work together to try to reach them.

CBT for treating BDD will usually include a technique known as exposure and response prevention (ERP).

This involves gradually facing situations that would normally make you think obsessively about your appearance and feel anxious.

Your therapist will help you to find other ways of dealing with your feelings in these situations so that, over time, you become able to deal with them without feeling self-conscious or afraid.

You may also be given some self-help information to read at home and your CBT might involve group work, depending on your symptoms.

CBT for children and young people will usually also involve their family members or carers.

Selective serotonin reuptake inhibitors (SSRIs)

SSRIs are a type of antidepressant.

There are a number of different SSRIs, but fluoxetine is most commonly used to treat BDD.

It may take up to 12 weeks for SSRIs to have an effect on your BDD symptoms.

If they work for you, you'll probably be asked to keep taking them for several months to improve your symptoms further and stop them coming back.

There are some common side effects of taking SSRIs, but these will often pass within a few weeks.

Your doctor will keep a close eye on you over the first few weeks. It's important to tell them if you're feeling particularly anxious or emotional, or are having thoughts of harming yourself.

If you've not had symptoms for 6 to 12 months, you'll probably be taken off SSRIs.

This will be done by slowly reducing your dose over time to help make sure your symptoms do not come back (relapse) and to avoid any side effects of coming off the drug (withdrawal symptoms), such as anxiety.

Children, adults younger than 30, and all people with a history of suicidal behaviour will need to be carefully monitored when taking SSRIs. This is because they may have a higher chance of developing suicidal thoughts or trying to hurt themselves in the early stages of treatment.

Children and young people may be offered an SSRI if they're having severe symptoms of BDD.

Medicine should only be suggested after they have seen a psychiatrist and been offered talking therapies.

Further treatment

If treatment with both CBT and an SSRI has not improved your BDD symptoms after 12 weeks, you may be prescribed a different type of SSRI or another antidepressant called clomipramine.

If you do not see any improvements in your symptoms, you may be referred to a mental health clinic or hospital that specialises in BDD, such as the National OCD/BDD Service in London.

These services will probably do a more in-depth assessment of your BDD.

They may offer you more CBT or a different kind of therapy, as well as a different kind of antidepressant.

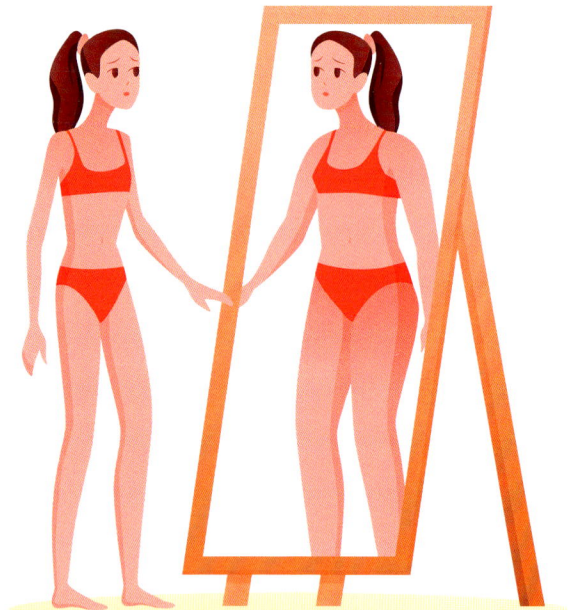

Causes of body dysmorphic disorder (BDD)

It's not known exactly what causes body dysmorphic disorder (BDD), but it might be associated with:

- genetics – you may be more likely to develop BDD if you have a relative with BDD, obsessive compulsive disorder (OCD) or depression
- a chemical imbalance in the brain
- a traumatic experience in the past – you may be more likely to develop BDD if you were teased, bullied or abused when you were a child

Some people with BDD also have another mental health condition, such as obsessive compulsive behaviour (OCD), generalised anxiety disorder or an eating disorder.

Things you can do to help with body dysmorphic disorder (BDD)

Support groups for body dysmorphic disorder (BDD)

Some people may find it helpful to contact or join a support group for information, advice and practical tips on coping with body dysmorphic disorder (BDD).

You can ask your doctor if there are any groups in your area, and the BDD Foundation has a directory of local and online BDD support groups.

You may also find the following organisations to be useful sources of information and advice:

- Anxiety UK
- International OCD Foundation
- Mind
- OCD Action
- OCD UK

Mental wellbeing

Things that can help with your mental wellbeing if you have BDD include:

- taking regular exercise
- making sure you get enough sleep

Some people also find it helpful to get together with friends or family, or to try doing something new to improve their mental wellbeing.

It may also be helpful to try some relaxation and breathing exercises to relieve stress and anxiety.

18 October 2023

The above information is reprinted with kind permission from the NHS.
© Crown Copyright 2024
This information is licensed under the Open Government Licence v3.0.
To view this licence, visit http://www.nationalarchives.gov.uk/doc/open-government-licence/

www.nhs.uk

More than my mental health: Body Dysmorphic Disorder

For as long as I can remember, I've had body image issues. I remember when I was 10 years old and a family friend – an adult – told me I have 'childbearing hips'. A weird thing for an adult to say to a child anyway, but it made me, at such a young age, become incredibly aware of what my body looked like. I remember when I was 12 and was the first person in my class to have to wear a bra because I'd suddenly 'developed'. And then I remember just as quickly stopping wearing it because the boys used to try and ping the straps open and it made me so uncomfortable and embarrassed.

I remember my first stretch marks. My first bit of cellulite. Being on diets, obsessing over every single calorie I took in. Losing pounds, gaining back those pounds. Gaining muscle, losing muscle. I remember when my first real relationship ended, I lost two and a half stone and everyone said I looked 'so skinny' and I thought it was ~GREAT~ but the reality was I was incredibly heartbroken, not eating, not taking care of myself, and in a really bad mental space.

I remember every time I've grabbed a cushion when I've sat on a sofa to 'hide my stomach' because I didn't want anyone to see what it looked like in that position. Every time I've cried because an outfit 'makes me look like a slug'. Every intimate moment I've ruined because I was too caught up in how I thought I looked. Every day at the beach I roasted under layers because I was too self conscious to wear a bikini. Every time I've had to manically fix my hair because it 'didn't look perfect'. Every time I've ripped my nail beds to shreds because I needed to 'just get that tiny bit of skin smooth'. I remember spending 99% of my time preoccupied with negative, hurtful, broken-record-type thoughts about the way I look, meaning more than who I actually am.

And I remember when it all changed. Last summer, I was out with two of my best friends, and, as the conversation typically goes, we ended up talking about body image. One of my friends said 'there must be something you love about how you look though?' and honestly, I struggled for an answer. And then, a week later, when me and my boyfriend were supposed to meet some friends for drinks, I had a full blown panic attack at the thought of it. I could barely breathe, I couldn't stop crying. And I knew this wasn't normal. Sure, most of my friends have some issue with the way they look sometimes, but none of them were a couple of minutes away from having to call an ambulance because of it. My boyfriend has always been very supportive of me, and has asked me several times in the years we've been together whether I've thought about talking to someone about my body image issues, but I always thought it was a pointless idea. On this day, once I'd got my breathing back, I told him he was right, and that I needed help.

I ended up using the NHS IAPT service, which offers free psychological therapies to people who need it. I had to fill out a form online, then got a call from a triage nurse. They went through some more questions, and a week later I

> When I was 10 years old ... a family friend – an adult – told me I have 'childbearing hips'.

heard back from them again. They had two options for me – get on a waiting list for in-person therapy (which could take up to 16 weeks) or start virtual therapy the following week. I chose the latter, and within a week I was having therapy for Intensive Body Dysmorphic Disorder. I didn't even know that's actually what I had until I spoke to the triage nurse, who told me that the symptoms I'd described were severe.

I had 16 weeks of therapy in total, with an incredible therapist called Nina. The type of therapy I had touched lightly on the reasons this behaviour started, but mostly on ways to change my thinking and combat the issues that overwhelmed me. For the first time in my life, I started to get a grasp of what this 'thing' was.

I learnt the term preoccupation, which kind of does what it says on the tin – it meant that the majority of my time was spent preoccupied with negative body image thoughts. And that's true. It was debilitating. I described many occasions to Nina about when I'd be alone in my flat, watching TV for example, and I'd become so obsessed with how I was sitting on the sofa because 'what if someone came in and saw me at this angle'. I explained that I constantly check myself in mirrors, reflective surfaces and my phone camera – and got told that this is not in fact a symptom of narcissism, but a very common symptom of having body dysmorphic disorder; the incessant need to make sure that how you are presented is 'right', 'perfect', 'in order'. I told her how many times I had to change my clothes throughout the day or had breakdowns deciding what to wear because clothes that showed off my figure were too panic-inducing, but clothes that were too baggy meant that I also worried that people might think I was bigger than I am. I told her how when I looked in the mirror all I could see were flaws. And that when I had a particularly bad/negative thought, my first instinct was to go to a mirror… not to make myself see that I was overthinking, but to do the opposite; to give in to the bad thought and to say 'yep, you're disgusting, I knew it'. All these things, and more, I'd struggled with for as long as I can remember, and all these things I thought were normal. That everyone did them.

Nina and I set out a plan for the 16 weeks I would be doing therapy. I had to learn a lot of tools and practices to help me overcome the worst feelings, and manage the smaller ones. One of the things I had to do was become wary of my safety behaviours – these are the subconscious things I do that feel like they are helping negative thoughts, but actually just prolong them. For me, my safety behaviours included readjusting my hair, covering myself with pillows or baggy clothes, and checking mirrors. I had to keep a diary during the time I was doing therapy to see how often I was doing these behaviours and why I did them. From there, Nina and I figured out ways to combat those and look in depth as to why I felt the need to have safety behaviours in place anyway.

Another major thing I had to do was mirror retraining. This might seem silly to some people, but when you have BDD, it's almost impossible to look in a mirror objectively. You only really ever look subjectively; you pick out all the small details about how your body image is 'wrong', what your 'flaws' are and you let your inner critic take over constantly. So I had to learn how to look in a mirror. I had to – in the sessions with Nina, and on my own time – look in the mirror and say five things about myself that are objective. So, for instance, 'I have brown hair. I have two arms. I have two legs. I am wearing a blue jumper. I have blue eyes.' And then I had to leave the mirror space and that was it. For me it was mind blowing how much it changed the way I viewed myself. When you just look at what is in front of you as an object, rather than a bundle of feelings, it really silences your inner critic, and feelings of shame, helplessness and lack of self worth. I am now able to look in a mirror – even get changed in front of a mirror – without negatively criticising myself, or having panic attacks about the way that I look.

I also had to do exposure therapy. Nina and I created a hierarchy of situations that gave me anxiety when it came to my body image issues, going from the least (around 50%) to the most anxiety (100%). The situations ranged from doing video calls with no makeup on to being in social situations wearing dresses with bare legs, wearing a bikini to going out to eat wearing clothing that is tight and therefore showing

off my figure fully. These situations may not seem like much to most people, but when you're consumed with negative thoughts about the way that you look, and specific areas of your body, 'simple' things can feel absolutely enormous and unmanageable. Over my 16 weeks, I had to do as many of the situations on my hierarchy table as possible. The idea being to immerse myself in the anxiety and ride the wave. So, I did as many as I could. And it was really tough, but really worked! One of the biggest things for me was going to the gym in just a sports bra and leggings – it's something I've seen plenty of women do and have never ever thought I'd be able to. My inner critic has never allowed me to see myself as worthy of doing that. But I did. I chose to do activities that I felt would give me the biggest chance of staying there the longest – so mostly things where I was standing up, rather than being bent in different positions, etc. It was a very scary thing to do and I felt sick as soon as we walked in. I felt quite vulnerable and exposed throughout too, but I managed to stay there for about twenty minutes before it got too overwhelming. Twenty minutes more than I ever thought I'd be able to do. And the idea with exposure therapy is that you keep doing it until it becomes something that doesn't induce any anxiety. So we went again the next day, and the next. And now, I feel like it's normal to work out in those clothes. It doesn't mean I do it every time I hit the gym, but I know I can if I want to. And it's the same with the other things on my hierarchy. I didn't get to do all of them, especially the number one spot – wear a bikini – because my therapy happened during winter (!) but, I am going on holiday this summer and I will be wearing a bikini and loving myself for it. Because a bikini body literally just means having a body and wearing a bikini!

I have to be honest, Body Dysmorphic Disorder is a miserable thing to live with. It can really damage ideas of self-worth, appreciation and love, and take its toll on a person emotionally and physically. But it's important to know that it can be helped. Through my therapy I have learnt to appreciate myself in ways I never thought possible. I have learnt to see myself in a new light, and love myself more than I ever thought I would. At the end of the day, the way we look is the least important thing about us, and I'm glad I can finally see – and believe – that. I've put a lot of work in to get this far, and the work will likely continue all my life, but it's something I am prepared for, and happy to do. I know a lot of people might also be feeling how I used to, and I truly recommend asking for help. Have real, uninhibited conversations about the way you feel about yourself with your friends or family members, and don't keep it bottled up, as that never helps and just gives your inner critic more fuel to fan the flames. And, if you feel ready to, sign up for the NHS IAPT services. They are free and available all over the country, and have professionals waiting to help.

9 May 2022

The above information is reprinted with kind permission from National Citizen Service.
© 2024 NCS

www.wearencs.com

Male body dysmorphia is a modern epidemic that's only worsening

Studies have shown that the majority of men display signs of some form of body dysmorphia, while hyper-jacked actors such as Channing Tatum and Zac Efron have expressed regret over their unhealthy workout regimes. Are we in the midst of a male body-image crisis, asks Matthew Neale

If you've ever been trapped in a conversation about 'dream dinner party guests', you'll know the curious schadenfreude of watching people work out which aspects of their personality they want to showcase. The last time it happened to me, someone picked Jason Momoa and Channing Tatum for 'eye candy', alongside – who else? – Martin Luther King Jr. While we'll perhaps never know Aquaman's views on the Montgomery bus boycott of 1955, the conversation did highlight our society's continued deference to jacked, hyper-masculine bodies.

Tatum himself was in the news earlier this year for speaking up about his own physique, specifically in the *Magic Mike* films. Appearing on *The Kelly Clarkson Show*, the actor deflected praise for a topless picture from that era, explaining that the routine was 'unhealthy' and that it had required starvation to achieve his look. Last week, social media was once again obsessing over Zac Efron's body as an image leaked of him filming a new role in a wrestling movie. This is a man, you may recall, who has been open about his struggles with body image, diet, and taking so many diuretics to get into shape for *Baywatch* (2017) that he fell into 'a pretty bad depression' and suffered from insomnia. If the tide is finally beginning to turn in how we talk about the societal expectations put on men's bodies, it's long overdue.

Historically, of course, the stereotypical image associated with eating disorders and body dysmorphia has been of a painfully thin young woman – and with good reason. Women's bodies have been scrutinised, criticised and idealised by men for millennia, a power dynamic that has accelerated over the last century with the rise of TV and film, supermodels, Instagram – developments that ushered in a cavalcade of highly edited and stylised images, framed by and for the male gaze. It is only to be expected, then, that data and studies around the subject have typically focused on women.

In 2022, it's harder to make that case. A study last year found that the majority of men (54%) displayed signs of body dysmorphic disorder (BDD), compared to 49% of women. If those numbers seem startling, based on the visibility of body image case studies and campaigns both online and offline today, one of the main factors will come as no surprise: too many men are simply not talking about it. Worse still, in some cases they aren't even recognising that their obsessive thoughts about their own weight and body image may have spiralled into dysmorphia.

Sam Thomas, who started a charity in his mid-twenties called Men Get Eating Disorders Too and has written extensively on mental health and addiction, experienced both body-image anxiety and an eating disorder – but not in the order you might imagine. Despite developing bulimia at the age of 13, a result of what he describes as a 'trauma response' to homophobic bullying, Thomas says he had 'no real concerns at all' about his weight or size back then. It was only years later, as he was recovering in his early twenties, that concerns about how he looked took hold.

'A lot of people assume that eating disorders are all to do with body image, but that wasn't the case with me,' he explains. 'It wasn't really until I left Liverpool to move to Brighton when I was 18 and started making friends for the first time, in the LGBT scene, that I started to realise how bothered everyone was about how they looked.'

After developing into an incredibly thin marathon runner, Thomas started hitting the gym and became 'very muscular and defined very quickly'. He found he could eat whatever he wanted and burn it off later in a workout, which proved appealing. But while going to the gym is a positive part of his life now, back then it was a totally different story. 'I just kept swinging from one unhealthy coping mechanism to another,' he says.

One of the key reasons why body image issues in men may frequently go unchecked is connected to the type of male body shapes that are fetishised. The extreme thinness often associated with anorexia and bulimia will more readily draw concerned enquiries, while someone whose obsession with the gym is fuelling their mental health crisis is more likely to be commended for their commitment, just like their Hollywood idols.

'There's no one body image ideal for men, whereas historically there was really one ideal for women – the thinner the better,' says Thomas, acknowledging that things have become 'a bit more complex now because of trends in plastic surgery and Instagram'. While men often feel pressured to lose weight to reduce their gut and look good in skinny jeans, a simultaneous pressure is exerted to gain weight in order to acquire massive, vein-popping biceps. As both Tatum and Efron have been at pains to point out, that image is a biology-defying aesthetic straight out of a comic book, and no more realistic than a woman with a 16-inch waist and a J-cup bust.

'With men, there's been this very 'alpha male' look with big muscles, but on the other hand you've got this slender-but-defined look, and not much going on in between. I used to say it's like trying to walk right and left at the same time,' he adds. 'I think a lot of men did not know what to aspire to.'

Of course, part of the problem with BDD is that how bodies are perceived by others can sometimes be irrelevant: if someone has convinced themselves they are the 'wrong'

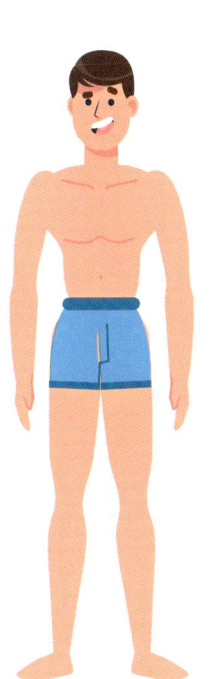 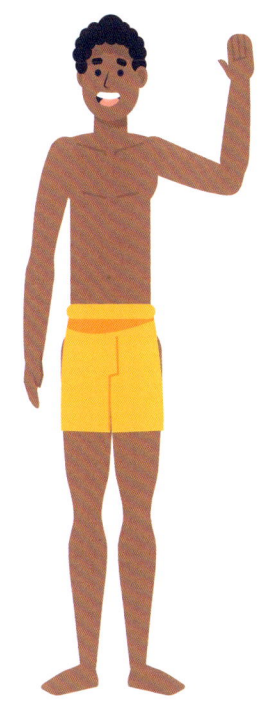 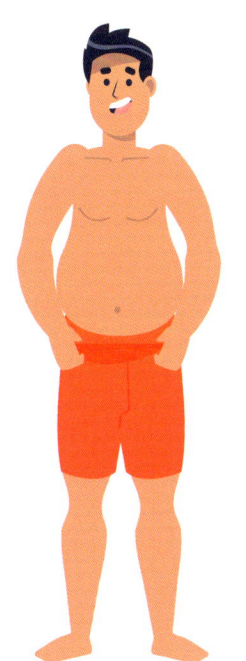 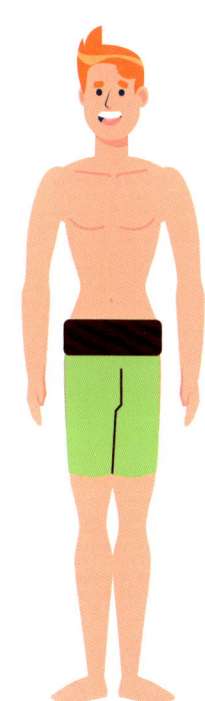

shape, the area of the body that needs the toughest workout is often the brain. Erene Hadjiioannou, spokesperson for the UK Council for Psychotherapy, says that finding out what dysmorphia means to the individual is essential.

'In psychotherapy you're working with someone's subjectivity, so if someone uses the term 'body dysmorphia' my first thought would be to unpack what that actually means to them,' she says. 'Where does that come from? What's perpetuating it? Because really what you're working with is internalisations of negative messages or what's socially acceptable, and how people carry that around and embody it.'

Gender variances don't just show up between cis men and cis women, either. For both trans men and trans women, the pressure to conform to a hyper-gendered body image can be exacerbated by the expectation to 'pass' as male or female in public; conversely, non-binary or genderqueer folk often speak about societal expectations of androgyny – that an appearance deemed too heavily masc- or femme-presenting might raise questions about the validity of their identity. It seems there's no escaping the feeling that our bodies might not be 'performing' in the way society would like them to.

While the temptation may be strong to simply tell people to 'be themselves' or 'be proud of who you are' – hashtag blessed! – it's worth remembering that there are considerable social rewards for people who ignore that advice and instead work to emulate everyone else's idea of physical perfection. If that sounds like the bleakest capitalist model of dehumanisation imaginable – reducing people to an assemblage of Botox and lip-fillers that improve your chances of attaining mental wellbeing and intimacy – well, that's pretty much where we are.

'I would describe it more in the ways our bodies are being used as currency, in a transactional sense, particularly in the early stages of a relationship,' Hadjiioannou says. 'It really takes away from the idea of ourselves as a whole person, if the focus is purely on what your profile picture looks like.'

What, if anything, can we do to try and fight something that seems so powerful and all-pervasive? The likes of Tatum and Efron speaking up about how utterly miserable and unhealthy their lives became in order to get 'shredded' for certain roles can only help, for sure. Thomas says he wants to see a more diverse range of male bodies represented, too. 'For women, there's increasingly a lot of representation for "plus-size" figures, but there isn't really an equivalent for men per se. We need to show men who perhaps don't feel represented that they are equally valid,' he says.

Some answers are easier than others. Today, we're all bombarded by mental health campaigns that implore us – particularly men – to talk more about our problems. While that's a noble request, perhaps we need to start thinking more about why men feel they can't talk about these issues; to ask why we are failing to build a culture in which people of all gender persuasions can feel empowered to raise their voice before it's too late.

'It sounds really cheesy, but the first relationship we have is with ourselves,' Hadjiioannou tells me towards the end of our conversation. 'If that relationship is healthy enough, that's when we can start extending it outwards to relationships with other people.'

That work involves self-analysis, of course, but it also requires us to continue unpacking the wider values of a system that rewards our slavish commitment to uniformity while paying performative lip service to individuality. Maybe then we'll start teaching future generations that 'eye candy' should never come at such an eye-watering price.

7 November 2022

Key facts

- 54% of men displayed signs of body dysmorphic disorder (BDD), compared to 49% of women.

The above information is reprinted with kind permission from *The Independent*.
© independent.co.uk 2024

www.independent.co.uk

Body image issues affect close to 40% of men – but many don't get the support they need

An article from *The Conversation*.

By Viren Swami, Professor of Social Psychology, Anglia Ruskin University

Lead guitarist of The Vamps, James Brittain-McVey, recently spoke out about the pressures he experienced with his body image. These pressures, which began when he was a teenager, led him to undergo liposuction at age 20. Speaking to a parliamentary committee on body image and mental health, he told MPs that he had struggled with anorexia since he was a teenager and that he still feels pressure to 'look a certain way'.

Brittain-McVey is not alone in his struggles with body image. It's estimated that between 30% and 40% of men are anxious about their weight and that up to 85% are dissatisfied with their muscularity. Many men desire a lean and muscular physique – which is often seen as synonymous with masculinity.

But without proper support, body image issues can have a major impact on both physical and mental health. Yet many men are hesitant to speak up about their body image issues – largely because of the stigma attached to it. Brittain-McVey also highlighted in his discussion with MPs the lack of support available for young men experiencing body image issues – which could further worsen poor mental health for those already struggling.

Mental health problems

Negative body image is more than just disliking the way your body looks – its outcomes can often be debilitating. Research shows that, in men, body image issues are linked with lower self-esteem, lower life satisfaction and a lack of confidence.

Body image issues can also lead to a host of mental health problems, such as severe anxiety and depression. It's estimated that around one in ten men have experienced suicidal thoughts and feelings and 4% have deliberately hurt themselves because of their body image issues.

Body image issues can also lead to disordered eating and muscle dysmorphia – an extreme preoccupation with having muscles. Exercise addiction – an insatiable craving for physical activity – has also been reported as a consequence of negative body image.

Not only can this lead to burnout and injury, it can in turn cause poorer psychological wellbeing and increases risk of developing an eating disorder. It can also have a severe impact on a person's social and work life, and may lead to other unhealthy behaviours – such as abusing anabolic steroids to build muscle.

These concerns have likely only become worse over the course of the pandemic. In a recent study, my colleagues and I showed pandemic-related stress and anxiety were linked with men's dissatisfaction with their weight and muscles.

Media influences

Many experts think the increase in men struggling with negative body image is due to the influence of mass media. Men often compare themselves to the hyper-muscular or lean models they see in action movies and health and fitness magazines. Because these comparisons are usually unrealistic, it increases the likelihood of experiencing weight and muscularity concerns.

In fact, reviews of research have shown that when men are exposed to idealised depictions of appearance in various forms of mass media, they end up feeling worse about their own bodies.

Social media only worsens these problems. Apps like Instagram are full of posts featuring hyper-muscular and lean men – and these posts often receive very high numbers of likes and comments. Unsurprisingly, reviews of evidence have found that men who frequently engage with these kinds of social media posts tend to have a more negative body image.

But it can sometimes be easy to over-emphasise the importance of social media – or any mass media, for that matter – on men's body image. Some research has suggested that the link between media exposure and negative body image may be very weak in men. Instead, it is likely that a range of sources – mass media, parents, peers – all contribute to negative body image in men.

Getting help

Body image issues are often viewed as a problem that disproportionately affects women – leaving many men reluctant to talk about their problems with friends and family or seek professional help. While men are increasingly encouraged to talk about their mental health, being open about body image concerns can still feel tricky – especially if men worry about appearing 'unmasculine' or being stigmatised and dismissed by others.

Health services can play an important role in helping men receive the help they need, but healthcare professionals are often hesitant to address body image issues in men because of a lack of knowledge, limited time and resources and inadequate training and guidelines on how to assist men.

Even when men seek help, they are sometimes dismissed or not taken seriously because negative body image is viewed as a 'woman's illness'. But when men are able to access preferred healthcare pathways for body image concerns, they often respond well to treatment.

Raising awareness more widely in society about negative body image in men is also crucial. An increasing number of men have opened up about their body image struggles – including other celebrities such as talk show host James Corden and actor Sebastian Stan. Bringing greater awareness to the fact that many men struggle with body image is one way of normalising the experience and helping men to recognise symptoms and seek help before their experiences become debilitating.

21 March 2022

Read
Read some articles by men who have experienced negative body image, such as by James Corden or Ed Sheeran.

Consider...
Why do you think that it is harder for men to seek help for body image issues?

Research
Have a look at newspapers, magazines and social media. How are men represented? Is there a variety of body types, or are the models or celebrities all similar body types?

Design
Design a poster highlighting negative body image in men.

THE CONVERSATION

The above information is reprinted with kind permission from The Conversation.
© 2010-2024, The Conversation Trust (UK) Limited

Exploring the dangers of idealised masculinity

Men are taught to be masculine, strong and to uphold the image of 'the perfect man'. Why?

What is the perfect man? Is he tanned with muscles? Is he blonde with blue eyes? Does he act rowdy, superior or dominant? Actually, he is all or none of these characteristics. He could be tall, short, big or small. He could have blue, brown, green, grey or any colour eyes. He could have scars or he could not. The point is, there is no 'perfect' man. There is no 'average' male. There is no one male image that young men should strive for, because perfection doesn't exist.

Not only does this cause issues with self-esteem and make men self-conscious, but it also affects their mental health. Millions of men worldwide struggle with body image that the vast majority won't talk about, that can lead to long-term mental health problems. In a recent survey, 55% of boys said they would consider changing their diet to get in shape, with 23% saying they believed the image of 'the perfect man' exists. Some of the main pressures to look in shape included coming from friends, social media, advertisements and celebrities. With men such as Freddie Flintoff and James Corden speaking out about body image in recent years, there is some hope for future generations to see themselves in a positive light when it comes to their physical appearance. But with these figures and pressures, societal changes are needed to prevent long term-damage to our youth and male counterparts.

Advertisements are guilty of warping our perception of image, with many young men believing they need to look the same as the men in adverts. Adverts from designers and brands such as Paco Rabanne and Armani, depict men as models or even gods to sell products. However, the use of editing, angles and excellent cinematography, make the men in these adverts seem 'perfect' and are used to draw people into both the advert and the product. So why is there so little representation of the everyday man in advertisements and in the media?

The lack of men in the media who haven't had make-up applied to their face to make them look vibrant and alive, or who haven't been airbrushed post-shoot, is shocking and increasingly damaging to young men, as it causes often irreparable damage when it comes to the way they perceive their own bodies.

Men should be proud and supportive of each other's bodies, whatever shape and size they are. Image should be seen as an extension of a person's personality and character, not the first detail you should judge upon meeting them. Yes, media coverage should be diversified and representative, but issues like body positivity need to be solved by starting small, with individual people and then spreading to all corners of society.

By forming ideas to combat idealised masculinity in all walks of life, from film to the workplace, pubs to schools, we can reduce and ultimately end male heartache when it comes to body image, size, shape and weight. By depicting men in everyday settings with no editing or make-up, no fancy lighting or finely tuned angles, the warped view that currently surrounds the male population will soon start to clear and they can move to the crucial stage of body positivity: acceptance. Once acceptance has been achieved (and it is truly a gruelling stage to fight your way through, and is extremely difficult when your self-esteem has been reduced to an atom), positivity and expression will flourish.

Male and female body image issues will always persist, even in the best of times and in the smallest capacities, but if we combat idealised ideas of masculinity together, we can stop the increase in the disproportionate number of young (and old) men suffering due to bodies that they can't change.

If we all lived the same, we would all still look different. So why are we judging each other?

6 July 2021

The above information is reprinted with kind permission from National Citizen Service.
© 2024 NCS
www.wearencs.com

Show don't tell: parents' role in promoting positive body image

This is how parents can help kids feel comfortable in their bodies.

By Charlotte Markey Ph.D.

Key points

- A new study found that teens desire acceptance, love, and support from parents when it comes to their bodies.
- Kids want their parents to be positive body image role models.
- A new book points out the important societal implications of teens' body dissatisfaction.
- 'The older generation, they made/reinforce the beauty standards, then pass it on to their kids.'

The last thing most parents want to do is contribute to the intergenerational transmission of body image concerns. We want our kids to be confident and comfortable in their own skins. But we aren't always sure how to accomplish this.

A recently published study titled, *Be more positive and more kind to your own bodies*, asked 14- to 24-year-olds how they would like their parents to support their body image. This survey of 652 young people confirms what body image scientists have been suggesting to parents for years: 'Promote body acceptance.' 'Provide unconditional love and support.' 'Be a good role model.' These were among kids' top recommendations for their parents.

It doesn't sound like rocket science, but, in practice, it's not always easy.

As psychologist Dr. Jo-Ann Finkelstein reminds us, 'Caring about how we look is a normal part of being human, but putting too much stock in our own attractiveness outsources our self-worth to others' opinions.' In her recent book, *Sexism and Sensibility: Raising Empowered, Resilient Girls in the Modern World*, she explores the sharp gender divide in not just body image but also the effort and mental space that appearance issues occupy. Whereas teen girls spend 7.7 hours per week on their appearance, boys are spending half that amount of time and, 'have permission to get on with their lives with a quick shower and comfy clothes.' This alone is a reason for parents to consciously work to socialise their kids to reject the demands that unrealistic beauty ideals and capitalist forces use to entice our young.

The consequences of body image concerns can be severe at the individual level: dieting, disordered eating, anxiety, and depression. But there are also broader consequences; gender equality itself is at risk when girls are tasked with a longer daily to-do list of hygiene and beautification routines. In Finkelstein's words, 'The beast of beauty culture is arguably the patriarchy's greatest tool for maintaining the status quo.'

In my recent book, *Adultish: The Body Image Book for Life*, I encourage readers to appreciate that our bodies are not infinitely malleable. It is a myth that 'just trying harder' can lead the majority of us to achieve the impossible beauty ideals that confront us. Of course, it is an appealing myth, because who doesn't like to think that beauty, health, happiness, and success are all within reach? And beauty, health, happiness, and success, of course, are often discussed as completely interwoven, which is also wrong.

And, yet, according to Finkelstein, it is impossible for adolescents in this formative stage of identity development not to feel like they are falling short when they are not flawless. The ubiquitous presentation of uncommon – nearly cartoonish – appearances on social media and 'solutions' for achieving these ideals is compelling.

Parents are brainwashed by these ideals as well and may have unrealistic expectations for their own kids. However, youth in the aforementioned study were clear that they did not want their parents to comment on their bodies, fat shame them or others, encourage dieting, or suggest that kids should be working to change their bodies. Most parents would never do any of this intentionally, but even subtle comments can stick with kids for years. One woman I interviewed for my latest book shared that all it took was her mom telling her she didn't have the body for crop tops and she resorted to wearing baggy clothes for an entire year. Parents may offer well-intentioned appearance guidance but, as Finkelstein suggests, 'The wish to save them from suffering can cause more suffering.'

I appreciate, as a parent, that it can feel overwhelming to try to confront the media, advertisements, and peers that contribute to our kids' body image concerns. Many of us may have our own body image baggage as well. But, according to kids, our greatest weapon against the forces that encourage their body dissatisfaction is to be a good role model. In Finkelstein's research, she found that body appreciation blooms when kids feel acceptance of their bodies by important people in their lives.

We can help kids feel safe, supported, and comfortable in their bodies. Their bodies will grow and change, but parents can be a constant in their development.

2 September 2024

The above information is reprinted with kind permission from Psychology Today.
© 2024 Sussex Publishers, LLC

www.psychologytoday.com

Body image in childhood

How comfortable are children and young people with their bodies?

While exact estimates vary, depending on how body image is measured, concerns and worries about appearance are commonplace among young people. One survey of 11–16-year-olds in the UK by Be Real found that 79% said how they look is important to them, and over half (52%) often worry about how they look. In our survey of young people aged 13–19, 35% said their body image causes them to 'often' or 'always' worry.

While body image concerns affect both boys and girls, research suggests that girls are more likely to be dissatisfied with their appearance and their weight than boys. In our survey, 46% of girls reported that their body image causes them to worry 'often' or 'always' compared to 25% of boys. Body image concerns can also affect very young children. One review found studies identifying body dissatisfaction in children under the age of six, though estimates of the degree of dissatisfaction varied widely depending on how it was measured.

Young people also tell us that body image is a substantial concern, with 16–25-year-olds identifying it as the third biggest challenge currently causing harm to young people, with lack of employment opportunities and failure to succeed within the education system as the first two.

How does body image affect children and young people?

In young people, body dissatisfaction has been linked to risk-taking behaviours and mental health problems. One survey of UK adolescents by Be Real found that 36% agreed they would do 'whatever it took' to look good, with 57% saying they had considered going on a diet and 10% saying they had considered cosmetic surgery. Among secondary school boys, 10% said they would consider taking steroids to achieve their goals.

Poor body image may also prevent young people from engaging in healthy behaviours, with some studies finding that children with poorer body image are less likely to take part in physical activity, and survey data from Be Real finding that 36% of girls and 24% of boys report avoiding taking part in activities like physical education due to worries about their appearance. Among adolescents, research has found that those with greater body appreciation are less likely to diet or use alcohol or cigarettes.

Body dissatisfaction and pressure to be thin have been linked to depressive symptoms and symptoms of anxiety disorders such as social anxiety or panic disorder, particularly in those children who do not match societal views of the 'ideal body'. Some studies have found that weight and body mass index (BMI) are correlated with body dissatisfaction, with young people who are overweight or obese reporting greater depressive symptoms and lower self-esteem than their peers.

Research conducted with young women also found a higher likelihood of suicidal thoughts among those women who reported extreme weight control behaviours (e.g., taking diet pills, diuretics or laxatives), with an additional study suggesting that body image concerns may be a risk factor for self-harm behaviour among young people who are experiencing emotional difficulties.

What affects body image in childhood?

Body ideal internalisation

One common contributor to poor body image is pressure to live up to an 'ideal' body type or appearance and shame or other uncomfortable emotions when we perceive ourselves as not meeting this standard. The internalisation of this ideal has been linked to body dissatisfaction, disordered eating, and depressive symptoms in children and young people. These distressing emotions were reflected in our survey, where 37% of young people said they felt upset, and 31% said they felt ashamed about their body image.

This ideal tends to be different between genders. Young women often feel pressure to be thin but still maintain curves, whereas young men often report pressure to be tall and muscular. Children who rejected appearance-related ideals reported being more confident about their appearance and were least likely to report body image concerns.

How young people develop their sense of 'ideal' appearance is varied. Still, young people identify the media, pressure from family and friends, comparisons with peers, and personal factors like low self-esteem, feelings of depression, and a need for control as important influences on their body image.

The media and social media

One commonly researched influence on body image is exposure to unrealistic 'ideal' bodies through film, television, magazines, advertising and social media. Exposure to these images is thought to facilitate valuing these 'ideal' and unrealistic body types. One study, which followed 14- and 15-year-olds over three years, found that internalisation of these 'ideal' body shapes as presented in the media predicted negative emotions about appearance, which in turn predicted unhealthy eating behaviours. In our survey, 25% of young people (13% of boys and 37% of girls) said celebrities have caused them to worry about their body image, and 19% (10% of boys and 28% of girls) said TV shows caused them to worry about their body image.

Using more social media has also been linked to children and young people feeling less satisfied with their bodies. In our survey, 40% of young people (26% of boys and 54% of girls) said that images on social media have caused them to worry about their body image. One possible explanation

for this is that social media allows for negative comparisons with others based on appearance. This is something that has consistently been linked to body dissatisfaction. Some studies suggest time spent on social media is linked to the frequency of appearance-related comparison and peer competition, which in turn may be linked to body dissatisfaction and mental health.

Parents and family members

The influence of the media on body image may be lessened by parental behaviour. One study found that the relationship between social media use and body dissatisfaction was weaker for adolescents with more positive maternal relationships. Another found that the children of parents who reported greater control over time spent on social media reported spending less time online, making fewer appearance-related comparisons, and having a better overall mental health.

Parents and family can also have a negative effect on children's body image and increase the likelihood of difficulties in this area. One study of adolescent girls found that over half had experienced weight-based teasing from family members, particularly girls who weighed more. These experiences were related to higher levels of body dissatisfaction and unhealthy eating behaviour. This was also reflected in our survey, where 29% of young people (21% of boys and 37% of girls) agreed that things their family said caused them to worry about their body image. This extends to how parents think, act and speak about their own bodies and their children's bodies. Reviews of the research suggest that parents can affect their children's body image in both direct ways (comments or criticisms about weight and appearance) and more indirect ways (parental eating behaviours and attitudes toward their own bodies and appearance).

Peers

As children grow older, their peers begin to play more of a role in reinforcing what an ideal body looks like. This can be through pressure from friends to feel accepted. In our survey, 40% of young people (37% of boys and 42% of girls) agreed that things their friends said caused them to worry about their body image. Another survey found that 68% of boys cited friends as a source of pressure to look good.

How adolescents' bodies change during puberty (a time of change in body height, weight and shape), how this compares with their peers, and how it compares to their own ideas of what an 'ideal' body looks like (which, in turn, can be influenced by the factors outlined above) will therefore affect body image. This may be especially true for girls who mature earlier than their peers and boys who mature later than their peers.

The influence of peers can also be felt through bullying. A survey by Be Real of UK 11–16-year-olds found that over half of young people had experienced appearance-based bullying, with 40% of those young people experiencing bullying at least once a week and 54% saying the bullying had started by age 10. Children who do not match body ideals may be more likely to be the target of bullying. One review of the research found that young people who are overweight or obese are more likely to be subject to bullying than their peers.

Appearance-based bullying can be detrimental to children's mental health and body image. Adolescents who were cyberbullied were twice as likely to consider themselves 'too fat', and of those who were bullied about their appearance, 53% felt anxious, and 29% felt depressed. In contrast, having supportive friendships may be a protective influence. Some studies have found support for strong friendships being associated with decreased body dissatisfaction. However, children who are already feeling down about their bodies may perceive their peers as having a greater influence, particularly as self-esteem and body image are closely linked.

2022

Summarise

Write a short summary of this article and choose 3 key facts that stand out to you.

The above information is reprinted with kind permission from The Mental Health Foundation.
© 2024 The Mental Health Foundation

www.mentalhealth.org.uk

Body Image and The Media

Chapter 2

Children and negative body image: are filters to blame?

Warning: this blog contains discussions of mental health, self-harm, eating disorders and body issues in children which may cause distress.

By Nichola Hunter-Warburton

An influx of hyper-realistic face and body filters has taken the world by storm, causing a surge in the usage of face editing apps and face altering trends across all social media platforms. With children and young people becoming more addicted to social media than ever before, this poses the question; what impact are image altering filters having on children's perception of body image?

The ability to edit an image or video within an app is now readily available on many social media platforms. Some filters can be experimented with, adding humorous masks or props to alter an image or video. For many this is an innocent and fun pastime and may not be a usual cause for concern. However, the use of these filters may be having a more sinister impact on the lives of children and young people, as more and more filters are being developed to improve or alter a person's physical appearance.

When someone uses a filter, it is not always obvious; for instance, there are apps available that let the user alter their appearance during a livestream or video conversation. This could be extremely damaging to young viewers as they may not be aware that the person they are watching or speaking to is using a hyper-realistic filter, therefore making them believe that they are looking at a true representation of that person's face and body. This can lead to children and young people feeling inadequate compared to who they 'see' online.

In a recent online nationwide study, The Harris Poll found that 69% of parents of children under the age of 18 believe that social media image altering apps and filters negatively affect their children's body image. The survey was done on behalf of 'On Our Sleeves Movement' for children's mental health.

How are filters impacting young people's mental health?

A staggering three out of four teenagers feel shame and dislike towards their bodies, and children as young as 12 have admitted they feel unhappy with the image they see in the mirror. These findings come from a major new study which highlights the risks and dangers associated with social media usage in children and young people.

Shockingly, nearly half of all children and young people in the UK confess that they have stopped socialising entirely, started exercising excessively, or self-harmed because they are frequently ridiculed or teased online about their appearance the study claims. This demonstrates the significant impact that social media and the usage of filters and image altering apps can have on children and young people's mental health and wellbeing.

According to a recent report nearly one in five teenagers claim to have body image issues, and 14% reported having eating disorders, such as restricting food intake, binge eating, and purging or vomiting. Also, four out of ten teenagers admit to having significant difficulties with their mental health. Despite this, only one in ten young people are accessing the professional help required. These results come from a recent poll conducted by the adolescent mental health organisation 'stem4'. According to the charity, children and young people are in urgent need of mental health support.

Since more children and young people are in requirement of professional intervention for their mental health, it is very likely that children's charities will invest more resources in campaigns that support children's and young people's mental health.

Risk-taking behaviours and mental health difficulties in teenagers have been linked to body dissatisfaction. A *Be Real* study of adolescents in the UK found that 36% of those polled claimed they would go to any lengths to be 'attractive', a further 57% indicated they had considered dieting, and 10% had contemplated cosmetic surgery.

Examples of how social media filters can impact young people's feelings and behaviours

- They often compare themselves to digitally altered and enhanced versions of others online.
- They may feel pressure to alter and share particular photographs and videos of themselves in order to 'fit in.'
- They can have a distorted view of themselves as they may prefer the 'filtered' version or online version of how they look.
- If they don't receive enough 'likes' or comments on their posts, they could feel disappointment, shame or embarrassment.
- They may start to engage in risky behaviours to deal with their feelings of negative self-worth and poor body image, such as drinking and drug taking.

- In serious cases they may engage in self-harm behaviours, such as inflicting pain on themselves or refusing to eat or eating too much due to feelings of negative body image.
- They may seek out 'quick fixes' such as unregulated 'diet pills' or 'weight-loss shakes' or attempt to access illegal or unauthorised 'clinics' that offer dangerous body altering enhancements or procedures.

Why are filters so popular amongst children and young people?

The years between eight and 12 are critical ages for the social and emotional development of children. At this stage in life, they start looking for social networks outside of their parents, and online and offline friendships start to become more important.

By using online filters and editing apps, children and young people can change how they look with a simple touch of a button. With various filters from dog faces, bunnies and funny facial expressions to glamorous make up and fresh-faced beauty filters, there is no limit on what kind of filters can be accessed online and via social media apps. Although many filters provide light-hearted entertainment, the 'hyper-realistic' filter's emergence has created a new threat to young people's self-esteem and body image.

Studies with teenagers revealed that males typically tend to use filters for fun and entertainment purposes, whereas females use filters to make themselves appear 'prettier' and to enhance their appearance online. Numerous filters can dramatically alter an individual's image by changing the skin tone, adding make up, changing the face and bone structure, portraying flawless skin and fuller lips. Giving a 'doll-like' appearance. This can be detrimental to a young person's self-esteem as they may start to resent how they normally look without these filters.

According to a 2017 study, only around 65% of the time could people identify altered images online. In spite of this, these heavily edited photographs and videos posted online have the power to lower one's self-esteem, encourage harmful habits like binge eating or excessive exercise, and alter how a child perceives their identity. Based on this, it has been claimed that because filters alter the appearance of facial features, the message delivered to children and young people is that they are inadequate the way they are and they need filters to improve and change how they look.

How can parents help children with image and body issues?

As parents and teachers are not always able to monitor everything their children do online and may not be as familiar with the latest social media trends, apps and filters, it may be difficult to safeguard their online activity.

Here are some useful tips to help children and young people who may be suffering with feelings of negative body image.

- Ask them about the use of filters and editing tools, why they use them, and how they make them feel.
- Remind them that the majority of what we see online is a highlights reel and the real world is usually very different as we are not exposed to people's daily realities.
- Go through which accounts they are following with them and perhaps help to filter and remove any accounts that may be causing them to feel insecure or negative about themselves.
- Encourage them to follow body positive accounts, there are plenty out there that celebrate uniqueness and promote learning to love all parts of yourself.
- Remind them how great the 'offline' version of them is and help them to list their best qualities.
- If you hear them saying negative things about themselves or others remind them to be kind with their words.
- Be a positive role model, if your child or teenager is feeling insecure with their body image, you could suggest going clothes shopping together for a feel-good make over (charity shops have some excellent bargains that are on-trend and won't break the bank) or get them involved in some physical activity, such as a walk together or some at home yoga. Exercise produces much needed feel-good endorphins that can benefit you both.

Verdict

Although social media filters and apps can be damaging to the self-esteem of children and young people, not all of them are bad. Social media can be used in a safe, fun and enjoyable way which helps children and young people bond with friends and take time out from the stressors of daily life. Nevertheless, there is clear evidence to suggest that certain social media filters are contributing to reduced self-esteem and poor body image for children and young people.

However, by staying vigilant and checking in with them from time to time, especially if they are showing signs of low self-esteem and body image or are engaging in self-harming behaviours, being aware and talking to them about it can help to eliminate some of those negative feelings and will enable you to get them further help and support.

If you or someone you know is experiencing mental health issues related to any of the topics mentioned in this article, please seek medical advice or call 0800 1111 to speak with Childline or 116 123 for the Samaritans.

2 August 2023

Write

This article gives tips to parents on how to help their child with image and body image issues. What advice would you give to a friend that is experiencing these issues? Write 5 tips that could help your friend.

The above information is reprinted with kind permission from Little Lives UK.

© 2024 Little Lives UK

www.littlelives.org.uk

The media, fashion companies and the pressure of having a perfect body

Six in ten Britons think the media are promoting unattainable body image expectations, and eight in ten say the fashion industry has harmed appearance perceptions.

By Milan Dinic

The media – whether it's print, TV or online – is often blamed for promoting 'ideal' body images that contribute to unrealistic expectations and standards about the way a body should look.

The YouGov Body Image Study finds that more than eight in ten Britons (83%) think the media promotes an unattainable female body image, and nearly two-thirds (64%) say the same of male body image.

Among women aged 16–24, as many as 84% think the media are encouraging unachievable expectations of what a female body should be like, while 67% think it's the same situation for men. Although men in the same age group are about as likely to think the media is creating unrealistic standards for male beauty (68%), they are less likely than their female peers to think the media is doing so for female beauty (70%).

When it comes to the influence of fashion companies, eight in ten (80%) say that they too have had a negative impact on

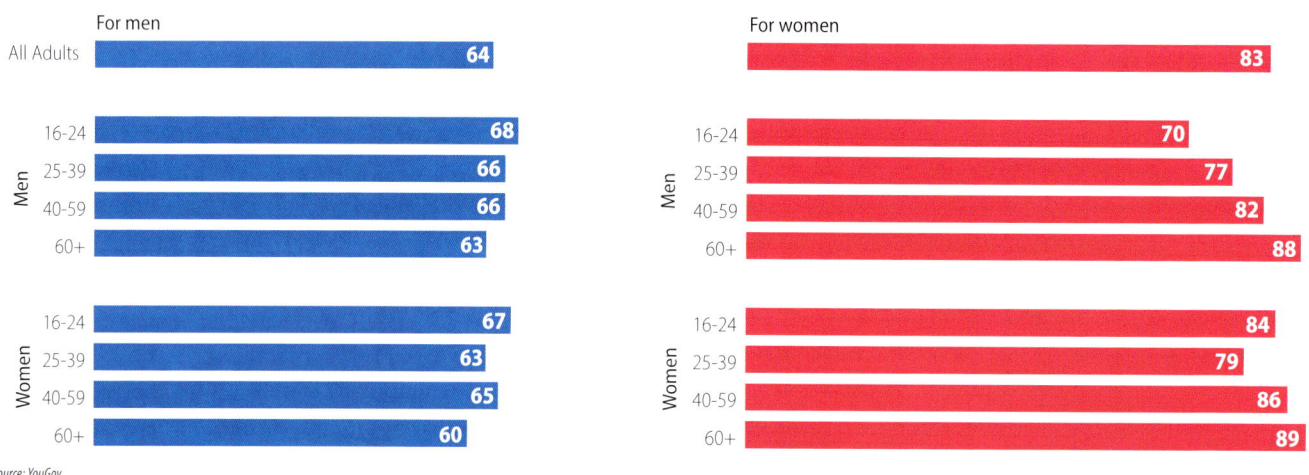

Britons of all ages and genders say that the media promotes unattainable body images for both men and women

In general, do you think the media does or does not promote an unattainable body image…? (% who answered 'It does')

Source: YouGov

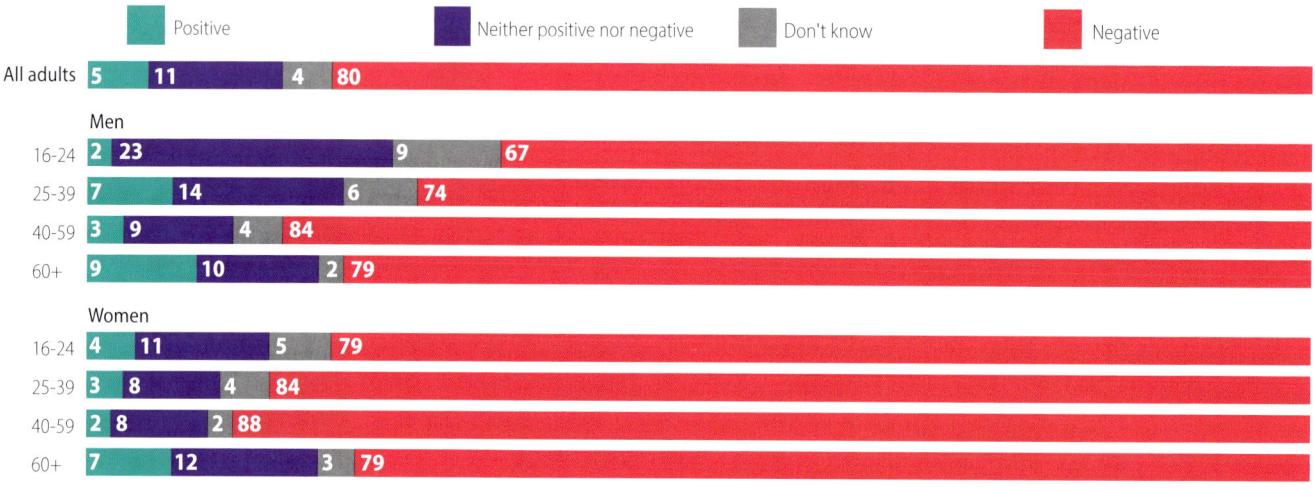

Eight in ten Brits say fashion companies have a negative impact on the perception of body image

In general, do you think that fashion companies have had a positive or negative impact on the perception of body image? (%)

Source: YouGov

Which gender faces the greatest pressure to have a certain body type?

In general, who do you think is under more pressure to have a certain body type? (%)

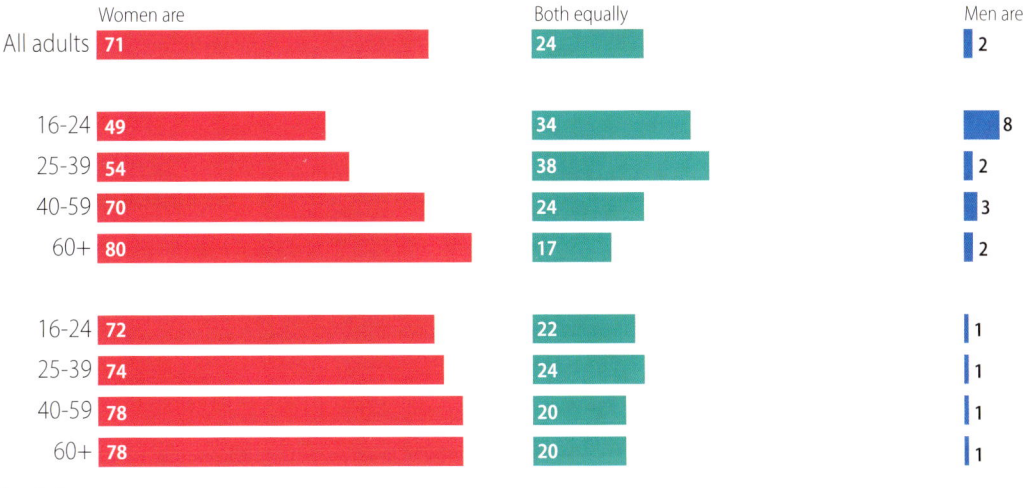

Source: YouGov

Two in five women under 25 feel a 'great deal' of pressure to have a certain body type

To what extent, if at all, do you feel under pressure to have a certain body type? (%)

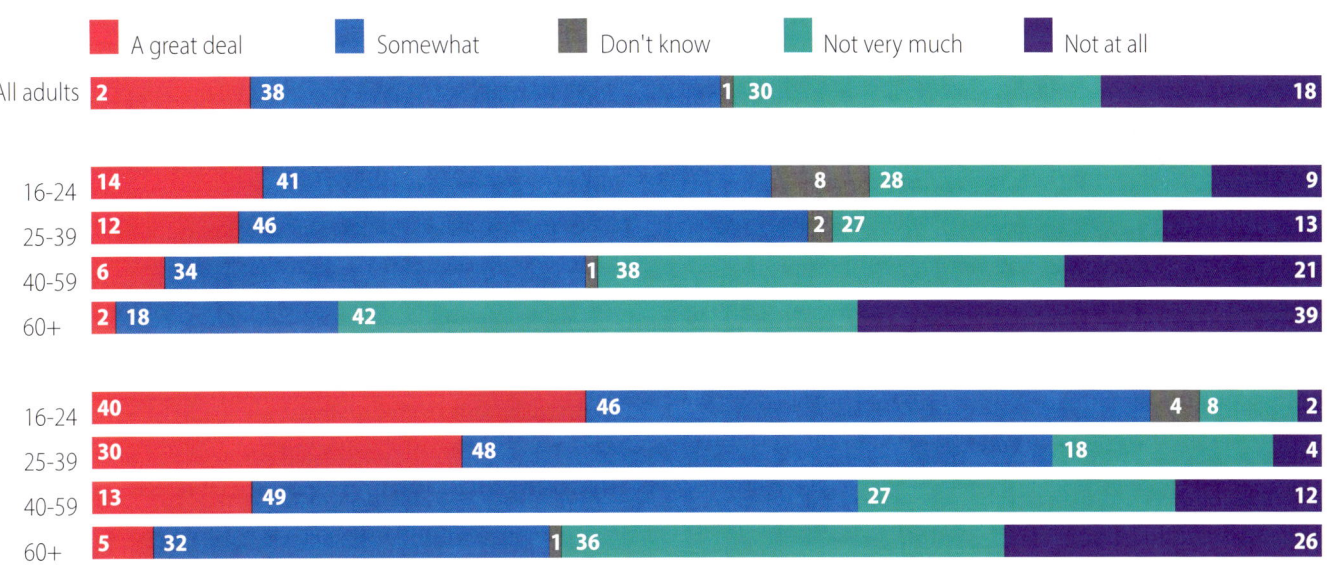

Source: YouGov

perceptions of body image. Only 5% think they have made a positive impact, with 11% saying neither.

There is a significant gap between younger men and women: 67% of men aged 16–24 and 74% of men aged 25–39 think the fashion companies have had a negative impact, while this goes up to 79% and 84% among women in the same age groups. There is almost no difference in the percentage of men and women 40 and older who share this view.

Seven in ten (71%) Britons say women are under more pressure than men to have a certain type of physical appearance – with 76% of women compared to 66% of men holding this view. A quarter (24%) of Britons think both men and women experience the same pressures.

Again, there is a very big difference in opinion between younger men and women. Among 16–39-year-old women, 72–74% say members of their gender are more under pressure to have a certain appearance. Among men the same age notably fewer (49–54%) say women are more exposed to pressures to have a certain body type. The gap narrows among men and women in their 40s and 50s (70% vs 78%), and there is no difference between men and women in their 60s and older (80% vs 78%).

Slightly more men (27%) than women (21%) say the pressure to have a similar body type is similar for both genders.

We also asked Britons directly if they felt pushed to have a certain body type. Half (51%) say they felt a great deal or somewhat pressured to do so, with women significantly more likely to say so than men (61% vs 40%).

Women aged 16–24 (40%) and 25–39 (30%) are significantly more likely than men of the same age (12–14%) or women over 40 (5–13%) to report feeling a great deal of expectation to have a specific body appearance.

Fewer than one in five Britons (18%) say they feel under no strain to have a certain body type, with this view more likely to apply to men (23%) than to women (13%).

5 August 2021

The above information is reprinted with kind permission from YouGov.
© 2024 YouGov PLC

www.yougov.co.uk

'Not much has changed': how fashion rules body image

By Tilda Gladwell

From London to New York and Paris to Milan, Fashion Weeks are being held across the globe this February. But these events aren't without their downsides, with eight in ten Britons believing the fashion industry has harmed their perceptions about appearance.

Despite the rise of the body positivity movement, championed by celebrities such as Ashley Graham, very little progress is being made within the fashion and modelling industries to increase size-inclusive representation.

The figures don't lie

Vogue Business releases a bi-annual *Body Inclusivity Report*, which calculates the percentage of size-inclusive representation on womenswear catwalks across the world.

The report for Spring/Summer 2024 reveals that 95.2% of models at Fashion Week were straight-size (that's a UK size 8 or lower), 3.8% were mid-size (UK 10-16) and 0.6% were plus-size (UK 18 or above).

'If you look at runways, not much has changed,' Ashley Graham tells *Mail Online*. 'If you look at designers, some of them are dressing different types of bodies, but it's not the norm. It's been this tiny crawl.'

While larger fashion houses lag in terms of size-inclusive representation, smaller brands, particularly those based in London, are the trailblazers in this area.

Baby steps towards change

Despite the tiny percentage of models on the catwalk who are above a size 8, the latest numbers are an improvement from Autumn/Winter 2023, showing that brands are recruiting more mid-size and plus-size models.

Nevertheless, the fashion industry has a long way to go before it can be called an inclusive place for ordinary women and models alike.

In December 2023, plus-size model Paloma Elsesser won 'Model of the Year' at the British Fashion Awards. At the age of 31, she became the first curvy model to win the award. However, shortly after the awards ceremony, she posted a message on Instagram to announce that she was 'taking a beat off [social media],' having received 'hate' comments online.

Positive change seems like a hard pill to swallow, for some.

Modelling's dark past

2023 became the year when the modelling industry's dark past resurfaced.

With the release of the *Supermodels* series, viewers were able to watch the rise of some of the industry's most iconic members: Cindy Crawford, Naomi Campbell, Linda Evangelista and Christy Turlington.

The four recounted their experiences of rising to prominence in the '90s, especially the adversity they faced to achieve international fame.

Evangelista gave the most candid view of the relationship between her career and her weight. Being told repeatedly that she needed to be thinner to be more beautiful, she went on numerous starvation diets to lose the excess 'fat'.

'I got to where I wasn't eating at all. I thought I was losing my mind,' she said of trying to 'fix' her body.

In 2016, she underwent a non-invasive cosmetic treatment called ZELTIQ CoolSculpting. This promised to reduce fat cell size. However, the treatment backfired, leaving her with unsightly areas of hardened fat clusters. Evangelista said her body was 'unrecognisable.'

When one of the world's most beautiful women is repeatedly told her body isn't good enough, what kind of message does this send to younger generations of girls?

By all indications, the expectation that models need to lose weight to get work and stay competitive is here to stay.

Statistics on models and eating disorders reveal that 62% of those who enter the modelling industry are told to lose weight by their agency or another industry professional. Over half (54%), engage in disordered eating or skip meals. And 81% of models have a Body Mass Index that is medically characterised as 'underweight.'

Unrealistic ideals

The idea that thin bodies with skinny legs and surfboard stomachs are the most desirable has been a persistent, and insidious, fashion industry standard.

In truth, the 'perfect' body is an unrealistic and arguably fluctuating ideal that is simply not worth starving yourself for.

Unfortunately, the majority of the media we consume, whether that's catwalks, magazines, or social media posts, perpetuates being slim and equates it with beauty. This undoubtedly harms many women's self-esteem. According to a study conducted by *ScienceDirect*:

'Women who are exposed to images of idealised bodies internalise the thin ideal and strive for an unrealistic standard of beauty, which can result in feelings of shame, body dissatisfaction, and low mood when they cannot achieve the same body type.'

In the US, 91% of women are dissatisfied with their bodies and 58% of college-aged girls feel pressured to be a certain weight.

In the UK, nearly half of all women aged 20–25 are unhappy with their bodies. This figure rises to almost 60% for those aged 35–40.

What about accountability?

Some use the monetary argument that it is just not profitable for brands to accommodate plus-size bodies. Following Victoria's Secret dalliance with size-inclusive marketing, sales plummeted. The company has now reverted to using its tried and tested 'Size Zero' template.

Others insist that the body positivity movement in fashion is equally damaging by normalising overweight bodies.

But I – and I suspect many other women too – believe the fashion industry needs to take some accountability for the harm it keeps causing women and young girls.

Deliberately hiring models below a size 8 ostracises the average woman and glorifies an unhealthy preoccupation with body image. It's time the fashion houses addressed their dark practices. Worrying about achieving the 'perfect' body should never become any woman's life obsession – or cause of despair.

Beat Eating Disorders provides Helplines offering support and information for anyone in need.

Call 0808 801 0677 or text SHOUT to 85258.

13 February 2024

Research

Create a questionnaire to find out people's views on the effect that media has on body image. Make sure you ask a range of different ages, so you can compare experiences of different age groups.

The above information is reprinted with kind permission from Shout Out UK.
© 2024 Shout Out UK

www.shoutoutuk.org

Social media is tanking people's body image

A new review, social media tragedies, and tips to protect you and your family.

By Alli Spotts-De Lazzer, MA, LMFT, LPCC, CEDS-C

> **Key points**
>
> - Social media use can contribute to body dissatisfaction in both adults and children.
>
> - Negative body image is associated with various adverse outcomes such as low self-esteem, eating disorders, and unhealthy lifestyle choices.
>
> - It's possible to become a more savvy social media consumer despite unhealthy content that appears in one's newsfeed.

Your social media may be baiting you to watch content that can exacerbate body dissatisfaction. That's according to a new review by Harriger and colleagues in the *Body Image* journal. Body dissatisfaction contributes to various problems, such as low self-esteem, anxiety, depression, eating and body image struggles, eating disorders, and unhealthy lifestyle behaviours.

While seeking positive body image content, you may find your social media feeds suggesting unsupportive, even triggering content.

How might that happen? Algorithms are basically programmed instructions, and those instructions are typically unknown to a social media user.

Think about your favourite social networking platforms. There are probably places that suggest videos, news, accounts, etc., you might like. Of course, any user could think that those suggestions are based purely on their interests. But in reality, many factors can influence what appears on feeds and pages. Examples include likes and dislikes (i.e., use of the anger emoji), shares, comments, time spent viewing videos, the company's goals and strategies, and more (Oremus et al., 2021). Harriger and colleagues point out that common social media algorithms funnel people online to 'personalised content that is often more extreme, less monitored, and designed to keep users engaged for longer periods of time.'

Which platform has the highest risk of amplifying body dissatisfaction?

It depends, and who knows?

- Algorithms aren't fixed or static. Harriger and associates point out the companies' lack of transparency about what's filtered into – or out of – your feed.

- Platforms that focus on visual images can be worse on body image than others that are less looks-focused (Vandenbosch, Fardouly, & Tiggemann, 2022). Try this experiment to see if this rings true to you: Take a few seconds, and consider the potential impact of Twitter vs. Instagram vs. TikTok vs. Snapchat, etc.

- The use of image enhancement filters and editing software can compound the risk of, for example, eating disorders (Wick & Keel, 2020).

The form of social media we choose can enhance our vulnerabilities to feeling cruddy about ourselves, which can boomerang into potential mental health struggles.

Here's what we can do to fall less victim to the deleterious effects of social media on body image.

According to Harriger and colleagues:

- Educators, researchers, and clinicians can provide media literacy programs, and education can help potentially reduce the negative effects of social media.

- Parents can role-model healthy social media use and discuss the risks of social media use with their children.

- Users can remain mindful of the manipulations that may be occurring.

- All of us can advocate for social media corporations to protect their users better.

Check your social media habits if your body image or mental wellness has plummeted.

With billions of social media users globally, you're probably using some kind of social networking app. Harriger and associates' article urges top-down change: 'It is ultimately the responsibility of the social media corporations to protect and enhance the wellbeing of their users.' But unfortunately, powerful businesses don't always do what's in their customers' best interests (Harriger et al.). And that leaves healthy management up to each user.

Tragically, some people will not be able to facilitate their social media use without deleterious outcomes.

- Between 2011 and 2017, 259 selfie deaths occurred (Bansal et al., 2018). So, yes, that means that people were – and still are – willing to risk death for that great shot, the hope of going viral, or both.

- According to Facebook internal communications, 'Among teens who reported suicidal thoughts, 13% of British users and 6% of American users traced the desire to kill themselves to Instagram'. (Wells, Horwitz, & Seetharamam, 2021).

- Research repeatedly shows that social media can be addictive (Cheng et al., 2021). As many of us know, either personally or due to a loved one, addiction tends to result in social, mental, and behavioural problems.

- One mother in Connecticut is suing Snap and Meta, alleging the social media companies played roles in and have some responsibility for her 11-year-old's suicide (Jackson, 2022).

Research and revelations will continue to emerge.

Unfortunately, scientific data generally evolves slower than social media grows. So, for now, here are five useful tips:

1. Honour your intuition and common sense about it (as best as anyone can amid the potential manipulations).
2. For safety, try to monitor your and your family's usage as best you can.
3. Utilise practices for safer online experiences.
4. Increase your social media literacy to mitigate the adverse effects of social media.
5. Reach out to a therapist if you need support or might benefit from therapy.

You are more than your body image, number of followers, a view count, or time spent on social media. Your wellbeing matters.

12 April 2022

Research

Celebrities often edit and manipulate their images on social media. Some of the biggest Photoshop fails have been committed by The Kardashians, can you find any other images that have been obviously altered?

Write

In small groups, think of five tips that will help to make your online experiences around body image safer.

The above information is reprinted with kind permission from Psychology Today.
© 2024 Sussex Publishers, LLC

www.psychologytoday.com
www.therapyhelps.us

The camera never lies...
...Well the camera doesn't, but filters and editing do!

Retouching and editing photographs might seem like a modern invention, but it's actually been around almost as long as photography itself. From its early days, people have found ways to enhance, alter, or completely transform images. Let's take a journey through the history of photo editing and discover how it has evolved into what we use today.

Early beginnings (1800s)

Photography was invented in the early 19th century, with the first known photo taken by Joseph Nicéphore Niépce in 1826. It wasn't long before people wanted to tweak their pictures. In those days, cameras weren't very advanced, and photos often came out blurry, faded, or too dark. So, photographers began using simple techniques to improve their pictures. One of the earliest forms of retouching was done directly on the photo negatives – large glass plates that captured the image. Photographers used fine brushes and pencils to fill in imperfections, sharpen details, or adjust lighting.

One of the most famous early examples of photo manipulation is from 1860. A portrait of Abraham Lincoln was created by combining his head with the body of a politician named John C. Calhoun. This showed how early photographers were already experimenting with ways to alter reality!

Darkroom magic (1900s)

In the 20th century, photo editing took a big leap forward with the invention of darkroom techniques. Photographers used the darkroom, where they developed their photos, to perform all kinds of edits. Dodging and burning, which involves lightening or darkening parts of the photo, was a popular way to create more dramatic effects.

One famous darkroom technique was used by the legendary photographer Ansel Adams, who is known for his stunning black-and-white landscapes. Adams spent hours in the darkroom, tweaking his photos to get the perfect balance of light and shadow. He believed that editing was an essential part of the creative process.

Another notable moment came in the 1930s and 1940s when airbrushing became popular. This technique allowed photographers to remove blemishes, smooth skin, and even change facial features. It became widely used in fashion and advertising, paving the way for the flawless images we often see in magazines.

The digital revolution (1980s–Present)

Everything changed with the invention of digital photography in the late 20th century. In 1987, Adobe released Photoshop, the software that would revolutionise the way people edit photos. Photoshop made it easy to perform edits that would have taken hours in a darkroom. You could remove objects, adjust colours, and even create entirely new images with just a few clicks.

As technology advanced, photo editing became even more accessible. Today, anyone with a smartphone can use apps like Instagram or Snapseed to apply filters, fix lighting, or even swap faces with a friend. With artificial intelligence (AI) now involved, photo editing has become even faster and more sophisticated, allowing for near-instant retouching.

The impact on society

While photo editing has made it easier to capture and share beautiful images, it has also raised some concerns. Heavily edited images can create unrealistic beauty standards, especially on social media. However, when used responsibly, photo editing is a powerful tool for creativity and self-expression.

In conclusion, retouching and editing photographs have come a long way from the early days of hand-painting negatives. From darkroom magic to digital apps, the desire to enhance images has been constant. As technology continues to evolve, it's exciting to think about what the future holds for photo editing!

Spot the difference

This photo has been subtly edited, can you spot what things have been changed?

Research

Some companies, such as Boohoo, no longer retouch their models. Can you find any other companies that are no longer using Photoshop, or other editing programmes to retouch their images?

Debate

As a class, debate the issue of images of models and celebrities being retouched. Half of the class will agree with the use of filters and Photoshop, and the other half will be against it.

Artificial Intelligence, body image and toxic expectations

By Edward Herbert

Since ChatGPT started hitting headlines, there has been growing concern around the sophistication of Artificial Intelligence (AI) tools and their impact on children, especially on social media. These programs have the power to control what young people see online or alter images and videos discretely. The consequences of this can be stark, resulting in the promotion of unrealistic body image and toxic masculinity. This can leave children feeling insecure about their appearance or exclude them because they don't fit the 'norm'. We explore the potential risks of AI on young people and how to tackle them.

AI-powered image editing

There is a growing trend for social media platforms to have filters and design software to include AI-powered image editors and image generators. This means, at the click of a button people can alter a picture to change the way they or somebody else looks. This could be smoothing skin, altering facial features, or even changing someone's body shape. In fact, the tech has become so sophisticated you can even create a completely made-up, and scarily realistic, image dreamt up entirely by machine learning.

On first glance this might seem harmless, but it can quickly become toxic. There is already a lot of pressure put on young people through the images they see in magazines and on social media about body image and identity. Being able to alter appearances and post it online could create even more unrealistic beauty standards and distort young people's view of themselves.

Algorithmic bias and discrimination

In fact, an eating disorder awareness group asked an AI tool to generate the 'most desirable' man and woman. The 'perfect' women had blonde hair, tanned skin, brown eyes,

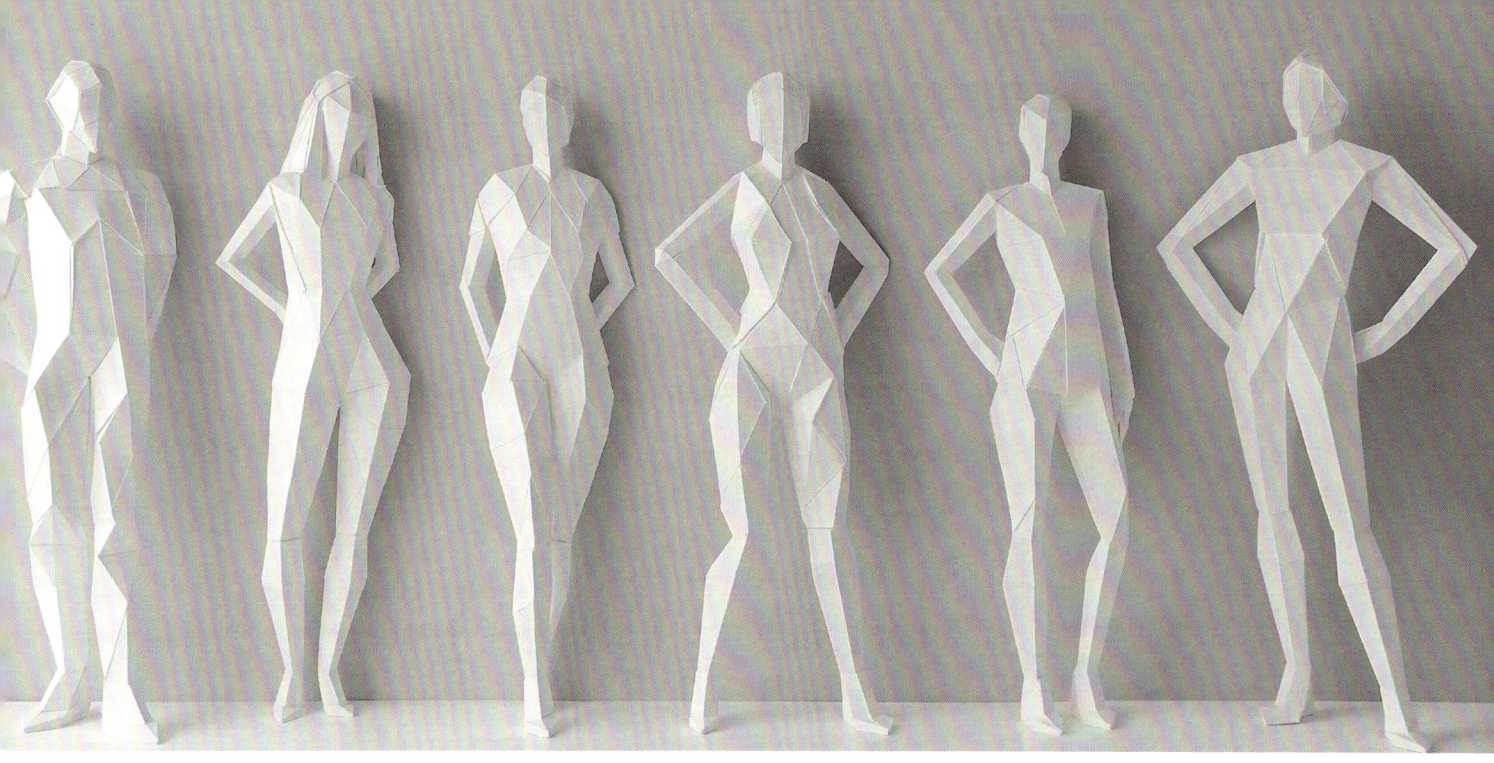

and a slim figure, while the 'perfect' man had chiselled cheekbones, brown eyes, and defined muscles.

What becomes clear from this is the over-simplification of what beauty is. The AI results pander to outdated stereotypes and reveal the tool's limitations and implicit biases. Algorithms used by platforms to recommend content often prioritise images and videos that conform to western conventional beauty standards. This can limit the diversity of body types and appearances represented online, making those who don't fit these standards feel excluded or inadequate.

Young people are susceptible to societal influences

Young people are particularly susceptible to societal influences and therefore more likely to strive for what is constantly being promoted to them. This can lead to stress, anxiety, and even depression as they compare themselves to the heavily edited and filtered images they see online.

On top of this, AI-driven advertising often targets young people with content that reinforces these unrealistic beauty standards. These targeted ads can heighten feelings of inadequacy and self-doubt, as young people are bombarded with messages that suggest they need to change their appearance to be accepted or successful.

Empowering young people through digital literacy

Young people spend a huge chunk of their lives on the internet and that isn't about to change. While we've outlined some of the risks, it isn't all bad. The internet can be a space for young people to connect, explore their identity and get their voices heard.

Protecting children from harmful content is important, but we also have a duty to help young people understand the platforms' risks and make informed decisions about what to view and how they view it. This should start at home, but also schools should be teaching digital literacy, such as critical thinking and appraising images.

The way we use AI and the values we teach young people will play a strong role in reducing the negative impacts. Children should be educated about the artificial nature of AI generated and filtered images, helping them understand that they often don't represent reality. Encouraging and promoting open conversations about body image and self-esteem can also provide the right environment for young people to discuss their feelings and concerns. Further to this, the focus shouldn't all be on the responsibility of young people. There have also been strong calls to force influencers and advertisers to declare digitally altered photos on social media.

16 October 2023

Think!

Both of the images on page 32 were created by AI, using the 'most desirable' prompts.

How do you think AI images may be harmful to children and young people?

Do you think that it is always possible to tell the difference between AI images and actual photographs of real people?

The above information is reprinted with kind permission from The Children's Society.

© The Children's Society 2024

www.childrenssociety.org.uk

New project to help young women deal with social media body image pressures

Young women navigating the complex world of body image on social media are the focus of a new project launched this week.

Researchers from the University of Portsmouth and The Girls' Network (Portsmouth) will work together with local young women to create a 'toolkit', to equip them with the skills and knowledge needed to cope with potentially harmful social media content.

As part of the project researchers will introduce girls to historic media content, including 19th and 20th century magazines and adverts, to show them that beauty ideals and body image perceptions have evolved over time.

Negative body image has become a growing concern affecting thousands of young girls in the UK. Media, advertising and celebrity culture have been highlighted as important influences on negative body image in reports from the All-Party Parliamentary Group on Body Image (2012) and the 2021 House of Commons report into body image. MPs and charities have recognised the need to equip young girls with tools to deal with the sometimes unrealistic and potentially harmful body ideals. The new project aims to create a way to help those who are often struggling.

Dr Helen Ringrow, Associate Head of the School of Education, Languages and Linguistics, at the University of Portsmouth said: 'Our aim is to build on existing work by creating resources designed to be used outside of a formal education environment, co-produced by and for young women. This project responds to the Mental Health Foundation's call for a media literacy toolkit, co-produced by young people, to enable them to better navigate contemporary messaging on body image.'

Previous research has found that young women's use of social media can help in connecting with others and staying informed, but may also relate to increased negative preoccupations with appearance, their body image, and detrimental effects on mood (Fardouly et al., 2018).

Dr Ringrow says: 'The previous research has not always focused on the role of language on social media – in particular the possible impact of certain words and phrasing which might be misleading, so this new research will include a language focus.'

Researchers plan to examine how young women navigate media content relating to body image and to co-create a relevant resource to help in this area. Researchers also want to find out if showing girls historic media content will help them realise that there are no fixed standards related to body image and that pressure on girls existed in different ways well before social media.

Through The Girls' Network, researchers will engage with young women in the Portsmouth area. The team will assess young women volunteer's awareness of how beauty standards are socially, culturally and historically constructed. There will then be a set of focus groups, leading to the new 'toolkit'. It has the potential to be expanded across the UK through The Girls' Network and will be participant-centred rather than teacher-led.

Paula Falck, The Girls' Network Manager for Portsmouth and Southampton, says: 'We are delighted to be working with the University of Portsmouth team on this important project, the girls are excited to be involved and looking forward to the first session'.

The first focus group will involve discussions around how the girls interact with social media and any challenges they face in terms of social (and mainstream) media and body image. In the second set of focus groups participants will learn about, and then discuss, historical media content (19th and 20th century magazines and adverts) in order to help them understand how the 'ideal body' changes across time and to show how beauty standards are not fixed. The focus group will end with a short task to check whether seeing historical media content has helped girls to recognise body image as something that depends on culture and time.

Dr Ringrow will be working with Dr Charlotte Boyce from the University of Portsmouth.

The University of Portsmouth team is also collaborating with Dr Stephen Pihlaja from Aston University on the project. Researchers hope the online 'toolkit' will be ready for use by September 2024.

16 March 2024

The above information is reprinted with kind permission from the University of Portsmouth.
© 2024 University of Portsmouth
www.port.ac.uk

Chapter 3

Feeling Positive!

Body positivity: embracing every body

In today's world, where social media and advertisements are filled with images of seemingly perfect people, it can be easy to feel like you don't measure up. Many teens find themselves comparing their bodies to the 'ideal' body types they see online, on TV, or in magazines. This can lead to negative feelings about their own bodies and even harm their self-esteem. That's where body positivity comes in.

What is body positivity?

Body positivity is all about accepting and loving your body, no matter what shape, size, or appearance it has. It encourages people to appreciate their bodies for what they can do, rather than criticising how they look. Everyone's body is unique, and body positivity teaches us that there isn't just one 'right' way to look.

This movement challenges the unrealistic beauty standards often presented by the media. It promotes the idea that every body is beautiful, whether it's tall, short, curvy, thin, or anything in between. But body positivity isn't just about how you look; it's also about how you *feel* in your own skin. It's about being confident, proud, and comfortable with who you are.

Why is body positivity important?

During the teenage years, many people go through significant changes. As your body grows and develops, it can feel strange or uncomfortable at times. You might notice parts of your body looking different from your friends', or you might compare yourself to celebrities or influencers who always seem to look flawless. These comparisons can make you feel insecure or unhappy with your body.

Body positivity is important because it reminds you that it's okay to look different from others. There's no 'perfect' body type, and beauty comes in all forms. When you embrace body positivity, you give yourself permission to love and accept your body exactly as it is. This can help boost your confidence and improve your mental health.

How to practise body positivity

Here are some ways you can start embracing body positivity in your everyday life:

1. **Avoid comparing yourself to others:** It's easy to look at someone else and think, 'I wish I looked like that.' But everyone's body is unique, and comparing yourself to others isn't helpful. Instead, focus on the things you like about yourself.

2. **Follow body-positive social media accounts:** Social media can be a tricky place when it comes to body image. Try following accounts that promote diversity and body positivity. This can help you see a wider range of body types and remind you that all bodies are beautiful.

3. **Wear what makes you feel good:** Fashion should be about expressing yourself and feeling comfortable in your own skin. Don't feel pressured to wear clothes just because they're trendy. Wear what makes *you* feel confident and happy.

4. **Be kind to yourself:** Everyone has days when they don't feel great about their appearance. On those days, remind yourself of all the amazing things your body does for you, like keeping you healthy and allowing you to do the things you enjoy.

5. **Surround yourself with positive people:** Friends who support and uplift you can make a big difference in how you feel about yourself. Spend time with people who make you feel good, not those who bring you down.

Body positivity is about more than just accepting your appearance; it's about loving and respecting yourself as a whole. By embracing body positivity, you can improve your self-confidence, boost your mental health, and help others feel good about themselves too. Remember, there is no 'perfect' body – every body is beautiful, including yours.

Body positivity – why women are tired of skinny stereotypes

By Ellie House

I am writing this for 15-year-old me, teased for having a flat chest.

I am writing this for 25-year-old me, at war with her post-partum body and newly rippled skin.

I am writing this for every woman who feels quite frankly exhausted by fighting her own reflection.

I grew up in the Nineties, where skinny was sexy.

In 1999, Victoria Beckham was asked to weigh herself on live TV after having her son, Brooklyn.

This was the era of Friends, where Monica was at the centre of fat jibes and Rachel was aghast when she learnt an acquaintance had gained weight.

'Hips or thighs,' she says, one hand covering her mouth in horror.

Fast forward to 2022, and there is, thankfully, greater representation both on screen and social media.

Women are celebrated for losing weight, especially when in the public eye.

Even celebs are speaking out about the pressure in the film industry, and labels above the UK average of a size 16 are becoming more common.

I recently went on holiday and opted for 'shaping' swimwear.

That is, until I saw women from other cultures, mainly German.

Stomachs that were not toned, strong thighs which jiggled. Glorious.

Age 30, I realised that my body was not made of playdough.

I've thought about body positivity ever since, defined as the social movement which advocates for the acceptance of all bodies, regardless of size, shape, etc.

I've spoken to women who are promoting the movement, and found out why we have a long way to go.

Victoria Mutch – Owner of Style for your Shape

Victoria juggles working in the oil and gas industry with running her own clothes shop on Schoolhill in Aberdeen.

She is passionate about promoting body inclusivity, with the shop offering sizes ranging between a size 8 and size 28.

Victoria believes that before body positivity can really make a difference, there needs to focus on body acceptance.

She has recently returned from a trip to Portugal, where she was discouraged from trying clothes on by a shop assistant who claimed nothing would fit.

A Facebook Live on the incident drew in more than 2,000 views.

'My body confidence is about an eight out of ten, I've worked hard over the past few years to improve that,' said Victoria.

'When I grew up, it was the time of The Spice Girls and Steps.

'Whilst Spice Girls were the first group to show diversity of character, they were all skinny.

'Now we have artists like Lizzo fully embracing how they look.

'We're constantly absorbing content on social media, but that can mean always looking at profiles of what you think your body should be like.

'That's what we need to check.'

Victoria launched her business to help people feel more confident, and the award-winning shop has proven popular with customers.

'People have the same body insecurities regardless of size,' she said.

'The body positive/confidence movement is great.

'But maybe it's too positive for where we are as a collective.

'We are very body negative, we need to get to the point of acceptance.

'The dialogue we say to ourselves is really important.

'When a company uses someone plus-sized in a campaign,

say Vogue, they are praised for it. Then things go back to how it was before.

'The change needs to be ongoing, it's about having representation for everyone.

'When I was on holiday and was told the clothes weren't likely to fit me, that could have really knocked me.

'The only reason it didn't linger is because of the work I've done on myself for the last four to five years.

'Some people will have had the same experience right here in Aberdeen, and that's just not right.'

Lisa Ross – Artist and founder of body positivity workshops

Lisa Ross, who is a mum of three and currently in her third year at Gray's School of Art, ran an exhibition last year to celebrate body positivity.

'Shameless' saw 50 nude portraits displayed to champion and celebrate every body type.

Lisa has since gone on to run workshops, encouraging people to look inwards at themselves.

'Why can we not just be ourselves?' said Lisa.

'I think women of all shapes and sizes are becoming more appreciated, I love that.

'Whether one boob is bigger than the other, or belly rolls.

'Magazines, for example, have been detrimental for so long, but we are slowly seeing changes.

'You've got to remember that for decades it was all about being skinny and having big boobs.

'It's ingrained and expected of women 'When in fact you can be healthy no matter what size you are.

'I hope my children's generation will carry on the body positivity message, and show the world that they won't conform.'

Celebs promoting body positivity

Lizzo, Demi Lovato, Serena Williams and Anne Hathaway, have all used their social media platforms to promote body positivity and acceptance.

A positive body image can feed into everything, from physical to mental health and self-esteem.

How we talk about our body around our children can also influence their own relationship with their appearance, and in turn with food.

16 October 2022

Design

Design a poster promoting body positivity, and give tips on how to be confident in your body.

The above information is reprinted with kind permission from *Press and Journal*.
© Aberdeen Journals Ltd 2024

www.pressandjournal.co.uk

Where is the male body positivity movement?

By Jacob Hawley

Last week I had a sickness bug. A few days of not eating, everything coming out and nothing going in, left me grey round the eyes and a bit green around the face.

I looked awful – and I worried about coming out of this and going straight into a few days of filming for a new football series I'm recording.

And yet, when I mentioned this to the lads I was working with, nearly everyone was confused about why I thought three days without eating would be a net-negative for my appearance.

Among the approving comments were: 'I bet your abs have come through though!', 'You're beach body ready now, mate!', 'You can probably avoid cardio this week!'

I'd forgotten, of course, that at this time of year, as the daffodils flower, the clocks change and airlines start spamming your inbox with cheap flights, many lads my age are having the same thoughts – 'I need to look like I'm auditioning for *Love Island*, and I need to do it fast'.

It's strange that while many women seem to be embracing body positivity and making efforts to detangle the mess caused by the negative image trends of the noughties, the pressure on men to look a certain way has ramped up.

Gyms are flooded with poor men like me, killing themselves to grow pecs; Instagram has seen a boom in fitness influencers popping up and making an industry from insecurities; and the supplement market has grown to the point that you can bulk, shred, grow, shrink, wake up, go to sleep, even get better at video games, all with the help of a milkshake that tastes like sick.

None of this is new, of course, but it does seem to have crept much further into the mainstream in recent years.

Growing up I was a skinny kid, a lanky beanpole of a teenager with long limbs and narrow shoulders and I hated it.

No-one told me this is what teenagers are supposed to look like – you are still developing, different things grow at different rates, and unfortunately your body isn't aware of how inconvenient this is for you as you try to snog people for the first time.

I wish I could go back and tell myself 'be patient, enjoy being a kid for a bit longer, in time you'll miss the fast metabolism that is making you this skinny'.

Rather than being patient with myself I saved up my money and bought a load of weights from Argos, setting up a home gym system where I'd roll a barbell off my bed and into my hands to do bench presses (more than once it nearly fell through the floor), all the while spending hours searching the internet for nutrition hacks that would help me put on weight.

And I wasn't alone among my peers – one mate covered his walls in paper and each morning would measure a different part of his body with tape to ensure that his fitness routine was making his limbs bigger, while another would add a tin of tuna to his protein shakes to create a disgusting chocolate fish medley that gave him an extra 20 grams of protein each morning.

At the time I never considered it unhealthy, and even looking back I don't know if I'd quite define our habits as eating disorders, but we were maintaining some mad routines.

Things didn't change when I got to university – I remember one particularly skinny bloke on my course trying a diet he found online that basically instructed him to drink a gallon of milk a day.

He didn't grow the shoulders he dreamed of, but he did fail most of his exams due to spending more time in the toilet than his lectures.

It's no wonder really that the fitness industry has exploded the way it has, when you look back at how many men of my generation obsessed over their bodies growing up. The demand has always been there; we were actively looking for the diet plans, the workout regimes, the supplements – we just didn't know how and where to find them.

Nowadays that poor kid who spent his whole student loan on full fat milk would spend it on a subscription to a men's magazine, a barrel of pancake batter flavoured whey protein and a pair of leggings with something like 'GYM RAT' emblazoned on the a**e.

And there isn't just an ugly industry profiteering on our desire to get sexy, influencers are popping up all over social media to try to gain traction from our fear of flab, usually with something to sell us.

Of course there's nothing wrong with someone who wants to dedicate their life to helping people get fit and healthy – and some of it is genuinely healthy, I'm sure – but some of the tactics seem a bit, well, scary.

There are numerous videos where quasi-scientific terms for starving yourself are normalised.

How have men's fitness trends reached a point of the borderline promotion of disordered eating when we've made so much progress on the awareness of body positivity around women?

Even as I write this, I know I'm not immune to it all.

My cupboards boast protein shakes and creatine, my notes app on my phone includes statistics of my workouts. Nothing has really changed since my mum picked me up outside Argos, aged 17, with those weights I'd spent weeks saving for (except I can now afford a gym membership, rather than rolling a bar that weighs the same as me off of my bed and challenging myself to catch it before it hits my skull).

As we creep into our 30s, so many men of my generation are just as image-concerned as we were as kids, just as desperate for a fix – the biggest difference is that, now, there's an entire industry ready to pounce on our fears.

Perhaps in a few years men will have our own body positivity movement, a backlash to all of this pressure.

In the meantime, with the temperature rising and Marbella beckoning, many men will be hitting the gym, ordering those supplements, following fitness freaks and knuckling down.

26 May 2022

The above information is reprinted with kind permission from *Metro* & DMG Media Licensing.
© 2024 Associated Newspapers Ltd

www.metro.co.uk

How to deal with body image issues

By Dr Jake Linardon

Body image is a broad, multifaceted concept that we hear about almost daily.

It essentially concerns how we think, feel, perceive, and behave towards our body and its parts.

Whilst we should all know the importance and benefits of valuing and appreciating our body for what it is and what it can do, the unfortunate reality is that most people – both young and old – experience a poor body image or have a distorted self-image (also known as 'self-image' disorders).

No one wants to experience a bad body image – it doesn't feel nice to scrutinise and loathe what you see in the mirror.

Making matters worse, a poor body image is the strongest risk factor for the development of an eating disorder.

In this article, I want to focus on body image and provide an answer to all the questions you might have in relation to this topic, including the signs and symptoms of negative body image, causes of negative body image, and how to treat negative body image.

Signs and symptoms of negative body image

As we spoke about, body image is multifaceted; it comprises cognitive, affective, perceptual, and behavioural components.

The 'broadness' of this concept means that there are many different signs and symptoms of poor body image.

Importantly, signs and symptoms may be expressed differently across people.

That is, one person's experience of negative body image can be completely different to another person's experience.

Let's take a look at the range of negative body image signs and symptoms.

- General unhappiness with one's body as a whole or its specific parts
- Equating one's self-worth on the basis of what they look like or weigh
- Obsessively scrutinizing one's body in front of a mirror or reflection
- Repetitive negative thoughts about one's body that interferes with many life domains
- Refusal to look at one's body due to anxiety
- Perceiving one's body to be larger than it really is
- Extreme anxiety over gaining weight
- Making disparaging comments about one's body and frequent comparison of one's shape and size to other people
- Feelings of being trapped in a larger body

As you'll see, there are a range of different signs and symptoms.

These signs and symptoms are important to spot, because they've each been shown to predict many different poor health outcomes, like eating disorder symptoms, functional impairment, and mental health problems.

Causes of negative body image

When discussing body image, an important question that arises concerns how a negative body image is caused, or what influences body image.

There's no simple answer.

There are range of factors that interact together to influence or cause a bad body image.

Luckily, these questions have been studied for decades, so we have a fairly good idea on what causes a distorted self-image.

Let's review the five most important causes of a poor body image.

1. Appearance ideal internalisation

Internalisation of the appearance ideal is the strongest predictor of negative body image.

It refers to the extent to which one 'buys in' to the notion that being thin, muscular, or lean will bring forth value, success, and beauty.

We live in a society that values certain body types; men are expected to be lean and muscular while women are expected to be thin.

There's an unspoken belief that if you achieve the ideal body type, you'll live a much happier and more successful life.

People who internalise this (believe it) are much more likely to experience body image problems, as it will soon be recognised that these ideals are largely unachievable.

Let me tell you tent assumptions we generally hold towards our appearance. These assumptions promote the appearance ideal internalization.

- Physically attractive people have it all
- Who I am as a person depends on how I look
- I should try my hardest to look my best all the time
- When people see me, the first thing they will notice is what's wrong with my appearance
- If people knew how I really look, they would probably like me less
- By managing my physical appearance, I can control my social and emotional life
- My appearance is responsible for nearly all that has happened in my life
- If I could look like how I wanted to, I'd be heaps happier
- Society's messages make it impossible for me to happy with my body
- The only way I could ever accept my looks would be to change them

2. Self-objectification

Women who self-objectify their body are likely to experience body image problems.

Let me explain.

Women in Western societies are routinely sexually objectified; they are evaluated and valued predominantly based on their physical appearance.

Experiences of sexual objectification routinely occur in interpersonal encounters and mass media.

Living in a cultural milieu of sexual objectification can socialise women to engage in self-objectification, meaning that they evaluate and value their own body based on appearance.

This self-objectification can cause women to be extremely unhappy with their own body.

3. Body comparisons

The extent to which you compare your body with other people also influences negative body image.

Why would these comparisons cause a negative body image?

Well, when we make comparisons, we tend to make unfair ones.

When we compare ourselves with someone else, we tend to look at all the things we like about the other person's body.

In contrast, when we evaluate our own body, we tend to dwell on and scrutinise all the things we don't like.

This causes us to feel ashamed or unhappy with our body image.

4. Fat Talk

Fat talk occurs when peers talk about their appearance in a negative light.

We'll often hear young girls say 'I look so fat today, and I feel disgusting'.

Fat talk promotes a negative body image because it reinforces the appearance ideals and encourages girls to strive for these ideals.

5. Perfectionistic tendencies

Being a perfectionist can also cause a negative body image.

This is because perfectionists are never happy with their body and are always trying to modify it in a way that aligns with the ideals we see in society.

No matter how thin or muscular a perfectionist's body is, they'll always find a way to critique it and be unhappy with it.

Body image therapy? How to reduce a negative body image

There are certain interventions purely dedicated towards helping people overcome a negative body image.

These interventions are empirically supported, meaning that several research studies have proven their effectiveness.

Most importantly, these interventions are often used for people across the entire life-span. So, the notion that older adults don't suffer from body image problems because they are more accepting of who they are doesn't really hold and isn't what we see in reality.

Let's take a look at some of the key intervention strategies used in body image therapy.

Understanding the origins of your negative body image

Before you're able to successfully address any negative body image tendencies, you first need to understand why you came to dislike your body so much in the first place.

Body image therapy utilises expressive writing to help you explore the origins of your negative body image.

Doing this will help you better understand what it is that you might need to address specifically in subsequent exercises

Mindfully accepting your body image experiences

In body image therapy, you will come to realise that negative body image takes over your life – you constantly think about your body, feel negatively towards it, and behave in ways that try to stop this from happening.

What you instead need to do is be more mindful and accepting of these situations.

In other words, teaching yourself to focus your attention on the here and now, in a non-judgmental fashion.

Mindfulness is a way of consciously 'stepping back' and really letting those negative thoughts and feelings towards your body subside.

In body image therapy, you are taught how to be more accepting, how to engage in body scans, and how to effectively meditate.

Correcting your cognitive distortions

We generally have a negative body image because of some distorted thoughts we have towards our body.

For example, you might believe that your entire self-worth is dictated by how you look or how much you weigh.

Body image therapy seeks to correct these fault assumptions, beliefs, and thoughts.

It does so via a range of cognitive restructuring exercises, exposure techniques, and self-monitoring strategies.

Being kind to your body

When we are unhappy with our body, we are generally mean to it.

We don't treat it well at all.

In body image therapy, there's not only a focus towards minimizing a negative body image, but also on promoting a positive body image.

You will learn to value, respect, and appreciate your body and all its wonderful capabilities.

Body image therapy will teach you how to speak kindly to your body via positive self-affirmations, take advantage of all the impressive functions it can perform via behavioural activation, and, overall, teach you to love the skin you're in.

7 April 2020

The above information is reprinted with kind permission from Break Binge Eating.
© 2024 Break Binge Eating

www.breakbingeeating.com

Further Reading/ Useful Websites

Useful websites

www.breakbingeeating.com

www.childrenssociety.org.uk

www.counselling-directory.org.uk

www.independent.co.uk

www.littlelives.org.uk

www.mentalhealth.org.uk

www.metro.co.uk

www.nhs.uk

www.port.ac.uk

www.pressandjournal.co.uk

www.psychologytoday.com

www.quickanddirtytips.com

www.shoutoutuk.org

www.theconversation.com

www.therapyhelps.us

www.wearencs.com

www.yougov.co.uk

Where can I find help?

Below are some telephone numbers, email addresses, and websites of agencies or charities that can offer support or advice if you, or someone you know, needs it.

Anxiety UK
Helpline: 08444 775 774
www.anxietyuk.org.uk

Childline
Helpline: 0800 1111
www.childline.org.uk

MIND
Helpline: 0300 123 3393
www.mind.org.uk

The Body Dysmorphic Foundation
www.youth.bddfoundation.org

You can also visit your GP if you need extra support with dealing with body image issues. They will be able to refer you to counselling services.

Further Reading

Page 2: The Savvy Psychologist Podcast: https://savvy-psychologist.simplecast.com/episodes/

Page 28: MeaningFULL: *23 Life-Changing Stories of Conquering Dieting, Weight, & Body Image Issues* by Alli Spotts-De Lazzer

Bansal, A., Garg, C., Pakhare, A., & Gupta, S. (2018). Selfies: A boon or bane?. Journal of Family Medicine and Primary Care, 7(4), 828–831. https://doi.org/10.4103/jfmpc.jfmpc_109_18

Cheng, C., Lau, Y., Chan, L., & Luk, J. W. (2021). Prevalence of social media addiction across 32 nations: Meta-analysis with subgroup analysis of classification schemes and cultural values. Addictive Behaviours, 117. https://doi.org/10.1016/j.addbeh.2021.106845

Harriger, J. A., Evans, J. A., Thompson, J. K., & Tylka, T. L. (2022). The dangers of the rabbit hole: Reflections on social media as a portal into a distorted world of edited bodies and eating disorder risk and the role of algorithms. Body Image, 41, 292-297. Advanced online publication. https://doi.org/10.1016/j.bodyim.2022.03.007

Jackson, S. (2022, January 22). Connecticut mother sues Meta and Snap, alleging they contributed to the suicide of 11-year-old daughter who had 'extreme addiction' to social media. Business Insider. https://www.businessinsider.com/mother-sues-meta-instagram-snap-allegin…

Oremus, W., Alcantara, C., Merrill, J. B., & Galocha, A. (2021, October 26). How Facebook shapes your feed: The evolution of what posts get top billing on users' news feeds, and what gets obscured. Washington Post. https://www.washingtonpost.com/technology/interactive/2021/how-facebook…

Spotts-De Lazzer, A. (2021, October 2021). Get the Most From Your Mental Health Social Media: Be aware and proceed with care [Blog]. Psychology Today. https://www.psychologytoday.com/us/blog/meaningfull/202110/get-the-most…

Vandenbosch, L., Fardouly, J., & Tiggemann, M. (2022). Social media and body image: Recent trends and future directions. Current Opinion in Psychology, 45, Article 101289. https://doi.org/10.1016/j.copsyc.2021.12.002

Wells, G., Horwitz, J., & Seetharaman, D. (2021, September 14). The Facebook Files: Facebook knows Instagram is toxic for teen girls, company documents show: Its own in-depth research shows a significant teen mental-health issue that Facebook plays down in public. The Wallstreet Journal. https://www.wsj.com/articles/facebook-knows-instagram-is-toxic-for-teen-girls-company-documents-show-11631620739

Wick, M. R., & Keel, P. K. (2020). Posting edited photos of the self: Increasing eating disorder risk or harmless behaviour? International Journal of Eating Disorders, 53, 864–872. https://doi.org/10.1002/eat.23263

Glossary

Airbrushing
A technique used to edit photos. Airbrushing may involve the removal of blemishes or spots, changing the shape or size of a person's features, and may lighten a person's skin tone. These digital edits are usually done in a way to make the final effect appear natural.

Angst
A feeling of anxiety or apprehension.

Anxiety
Feeling nervous, worried or distressed, sometimes to a point where the person feels so overwhelmed that they find everyday life very difficult to handle.

BMI (body mass index)
An abbreviation which stands for 'body mass index' and is used to determine whether an individual's weight is in proportion to their height. If a person's BMI is below 18.5 they are usually seen as being underweight. If a person has a BMI greater than or equal to 25, they are classed as overweight and a BMI of 30 and over is obese. As BMI is the same for both sexes and adults of all ages, it provides the most useful population-level measure of overweight and obesity. However, it should be considered a rough guide because it may not correspond to the same degree of 'fatness' in different individuals (e.g., a body builder could have a BMI of 30 but would not be obese because his weight would be primarily muscle rather than fat).

Body dysmorphic disorder (BDD)
A mental health condition where a person is preoccupied with their appearance which they believe has many flaws. These perceived flaws are often unnoticeable in others.

Body image
Body image is the subjective sense we have of our appearance and the experience of our physical embodiment. It is an individual's perception of what they look like or how they should look like. It can be influenced by personal memory along with external sources such as the media and comments made by other people.

Body positivity
The ideal that people should feel positive and proud about their bodies, regardless of their physical appearance.

Cosmetic surgery
A medical procedure which changes a person's appearance and can be performed on most parts of the human body. Cosmetic surgery can involve procedures such as inputting breast implants, bum lifts, Botox and lip fillers as well as changing bone structure.

Exercise
Physical activity that helps to improve and maintain a healthy body and mind. Exercise can be as easy as walking, swimming or dancing, to more intensive activity such as weight training, aerobics or High-Intensity Interval Training (HIIT).

Filters
Many apps have in built filters to alter photographs. While many filters help to improve the overall appearance of a photo, some have the facilities to change a person's features, such as whiten teeth, slim faces, or add makeup.

Objectify/Objectification
To turn something into an object in relation to sight, touch or another physical sense. To 'objectify' a person means to turn them into an object, meaning that they do not possess the same human rights as another individual. The person objectified is usually dominated by another person, or group of people.

Photoshop
A term applied to photos which are edited using digital software, and usually refers to editing which is done using the computer programme Adobe Photoshop. Airbrushing is one technique which may be used when 'photoshopping' an image.

Rhinoplasty
A procedure involving cosmetic surgery which involves altering the size or shape of a person's nose. Commonly referred to as a 'nose job'.

Self-esteem
A term referring to how an individual feels about their body. Relating to self-confidence, if a person has low self-esteem they may feel unhappy with the way they look. Alternatively, if a person has good/high self-esteem then they may feel particularly confident about their appearance.

Selfie
The selfie has become a huge part of modern life. A selfie is a photograph that a person takes of themselves, usually with a smartphone or digital camera, usually with the intent of sharing it on social media. It has transformed the simple self-portrait into something more immediate and has grown in cultural importance – it's been linked to identity, self-exploration and narcissism.

Social media
Media which are designed specifically for electronic communication. 'Social networking' websites allow users to interact using instant messaging, share information, photos and videos and ultimately create an online community. Examples include Facebook, LinkedIn and micro-blogging site Twitter.

Index

A
abuse 4
affective body image 1, 3
AI (Artificial Intelligence) 32–33
algorithms 28, 32–33
antidepressants 9–10

B
behavioural aspect of body image 3
body dysmorphic disorder (BDD) 5, 7, 9–10, 11–13, 14–15
body positivity 1, 35, 36–37, 38–39
bullying 4, 21

C
causes 10, 40–41
CBT (cognitive behavioural therapy) 9
children and teenagers 6, 7, 8, 20–21, 22–23, 33
cognitive body image 3
cultural preferences 3, 4

D
diversity and inclusivity 1, 14–15, 18, 26–27, 32–33, 36–37

E
eating disorders 6, 7, 8, 14, 27

F
family 4, 19, 21
fashion industry 24–25, 26–27, 36–37
filters 22–23, 28, 30
fitness industry 4, 38–39

G
gender and body image 15, 19, 20, 24–25
Global statistics 6
gyms 13, 14, 38–39

H
help and advice *see also* treatments
    body dysmorphic disorder 10
    body image 2–3, 17, 41
    body positivity 35
    social media 8, 23, 28

I
ideal appearance
    children and teenagers 20–21
    and happiness 40
    men 14, 18, 32–33
    women 26–27, 32–33, 34
identity and appearance 15
image manipulation 18, 30–31, 32–33
inclusivity and diversity 1, 14–15, 18, 26–27, 32–33, 36–37
influences on body image 2–3, 4, 7–8, 16–17, 20, 21, 24–25, 40–41 *see also* social media

L
LGBT 14, 15

M
media influence 4, 7–8, 16–17, 20, 24–25
men and boys 6–7, 14–15, 16–17, 18, 38–39
mental health 1, 5, 10, 16, 20, 22
modelling 26–27
muscle dysmorphia 5, 6, 7, 16

N
negative body image 2, 40–41

P
parenting 19, 21, 23
peer pressure 21
perceptual body image 1, 2
photo editing 18, 30–31, 32–33
puberty 4

S
self-esteem 1, 4
size, body 26–27, 36–37
social media 8, 17, 20–21, 22–23, 28–29, 33, 34
sport 4, 6–7
SSRIs (selective serotonin reuptake inhibitors) 9–10
statistical information 5–8, 24–25
steroid and supplement use 6, 7, 38, 39
suicidal thoughts 29
support groups 10
symptoms 9, 40

T
teenagers 4, 6–7, 8, 20–21, 22–23, 35
treatments 9–10, 11–13, 17, 41

W
weight 5, 6, 7, 8, 14 *see also* size, body
women and girls 7, 26–27, 32–33, 34, 36–37